"I pledge to keep my body and brain active this summer."

_____
Name

20 _____
Year

Let's Get Ready for Kindergarten!

Summer Fit Preschool to Kindergarten

Authors: Kelly Terrill and Portia Marin

Fitness and Nutrition: Lisa Roberts RN, BSN, PHN, James Cordova, Charles Miller, Steve Edwards, Missy Jones, Barbara Sherwood, John Bartlette, Malu Egido, Michael Ward

Healthy Family Lifestyle: Jay and Jen Jacobs & Marci and Courtney Crozier

Layout and Design: Scott Aucutt

Cover Design and Illustrations: Andy Carlson

Illustrations: Roxanne Ottley and Scott Aucutt

Series Created by George Starks

Summer Fit Dedication

Summer Fit is dedicated to Julia Hobbs and Carla Fisher who are the authors and unsung heroes of the original summer workbook series that helped establish the importance of summer learning. These women helped pioneer summer learning and dedicated their lives to teaching children and supporting parents. Carla and Julia made the world a better place by touching the lives of others using their love of education.

Summer Fit is also dedicated to Michael Starks whose presence is missed dearly, but who continues to teach us every day the importance of having courage in difficult times and treating others with respect, dignity, and a genuine concern for others.

Summer Fit Caution

If you have any questions regarding your child's ability to complete any of the suggested fitness activities consult your family doctor or child's pediatrician. Some of these exercises may require adult supervision. Children should stretch and warm up before exercises. Do not push children past their comfort level or ability. These physical fitness activities were created to be fun for parents and caregivers as well as the child, but not as a professional training or weight loss program. Exercise should stop immediately if you or your child experiences any of the following symptoms: pain, feeling dizzy or faint, nausea, or severe fatigue.

Summer Fit Copyright

Special thanks to the Terry Fox Foundation for use of Terry's photo and inspiring us all to contribute to making the world a better place for others each in our own way.

Printed in the USA
All Rights Reserved
ISBN: 978-0-9762800-2-6
www.SummerFitLearning.com

TABLE OF CONTENTS

Dear Parents,

Without opportunities to learn and practice essential skills over the summer months, most children fall behind academically. Research shows that summer learning loss varies, but that children can lose the equivalency of 2.5 months of math and 2 months of reading skills while away from school. In addition, children lose more than just academic knowledge during the summer. Research also shows that children are at greater risk of actually gaining more weight during summer vacation than during the school year:

All young people experience learning losses when they do not engage in educational activities during the summer. Research spanning 100 years shows that students typically score lower on standardized tests at the end of summer vacation than they do on the same tests at the beginning of the summer (White, 1906; Heyns, 1978; Entwisle & Alexander 1992; Cooper, 1996; Downey et al, 2004).

Research shows that children gain weight three times faster during the summer months – gaining as much weight during the summer as they do during the entire school year – even though the summertime is three times shorter. Von Hippel, P. T., Powell, B., Downey, D.B., & Rowland, N. (2007).

In the New York City school system, elementary and middle school students who placed in the top third of a fitness scale had better math and reading scores than students in the bottom third of the fitness scale. Those who were in the top 5% for fitness scored an average of 36 percentage points higher on state reading and math exams than did the least-fit 5%. New York City Department of Health. (2009)

Summer vacation is a great opportunity to use a variety of resources and programs to extend the academic learning experience and to reinforce life and social skills. It is an opportunity to give learning a different look and feel than what children are used to during the school year. Summer is a season that should be fun and carefree, but do not underestimate the opportunity and importance of helping children prepare for the upcoming school year. The key to a successful new school year is keeping your children active and learning this summer!

Sincerely,

Summer Fit Learning

FACT
You are your child's greatest teacher.

Purpose

The purpose of Summer Fit is to offer a comprehensive program for parents that promotes health and physical activity along side of academic and social skills. Summer Fit is designed to help create healthy and balanced family lifestyles.

Stay Smart

Summer Fit contains activities in reading, writing, math, language arts, and science.

Program Components

Summer Fit activities and exercises are divided into 10 sections to correlate with the traditional 10 weeks of summer. Each section begins with a weekly overview and incentive calendar so parents and children can talk about the week ahead while reviewing the previous week. There are 10 pages of activities for each week. The child does 2 pages a day that should take 20-30 minutes a day to complete. Each day offers a simple routine to reinforce basic skills and includes a physical fitness exercise and healthy habit. Each week also reinforces a core value on a daily basis to build character and social skills. Activities start off easy and progressively get more difficult so by the end of the workbook children are mentally, physically and socially prepared for the grade ahead.

Stay Cool

Summer Fit uses role models to reinforce the importance of good character and social skills.

Stay Active

Summer Fit uses a daily fitness exercise and wellness tips to keep children moving and having fun.

Summer Fit includes a daily exercise program that children complete as part of their one-page of activities a day. These daily exercises and movement activities foster active lifestyles and get parents and children moving together.

Summer Fit uses daily value-based activities to reinforce good behavior.

Summer Fit promotes the body-brain connection and gives parents the tools to motivate children to use both.

Summer Fit includes an online component that gives children and parents additional summer learning and fitness resources at SummerFitLearning.com.

Summer Fit contains activities and exercises created by educators, parents and trainers committed to creating active learning environments that include movement and play as part of the learning experience.

Summer Fit uses role models from around the world to introduce and reinforce core values and the importance of good behavior.

The Whole Child philosophy is based on the belief that every child should be healthy, engaged, supported and challenged in all aspects of their lives. Investing in the *overall* development of your child is critical to their personal health and well being. There is increased awareness that a balanced approach to nurturing and teaching our children will benefit all aspects of their lives; therefore creating well rounded students who are better equipped to successfully navigate the ups and downs of their education careers.

Supports Common Core Standards

The Common Core provides teachers and parents with a common understanding of what students are expected to learn. These standards will provide appropriate benchmarks for all students, regardless of where they live and be applied for students in grades K-12. Summer Fit is aligned to Common Core Standards.

Learn more at: CoreStandards.org

Top 5 Parent Summer Tips

1 Routine: Set a time and a place for your child to complete their activities and exercises each day.

2 Balance: Use a combination of resources to reinforce basic skills in fun ways. Integrate technology with traditional learning, but do not replace one with another.

3 Motivate and Encourage: Inspire your child to complete their daily activities and exercises. Get excited and show your support of their accomplishments!

4 Play as a Family: Slap "high 5," jump up and down and get silly! Show how fun it is to be active by doing it yourself! Health Experts recommend 60 minutes of play a day and kids love seeing parents playing and having fun!

5 Eat Healthy (and together): Kids are more likely to eat less healthy during the summer, than during the school year. Put food back on the table and eat together at least once a day.

Physical activity is critical to your child's health and well-being. Research shows that children with better health are in school more days, learn better, have higher self esteem and lower risk of developing chronic diseases.

Exercise Provides:

✔ Stronger muscles and bones

✔ Leaner body because exercise helps control body fat

✔ Increased blood flow to the brain and wellness at home

✔ Lower blood pressure and blood cholesterol levels

✔ Kids who are active are less likely to develop weight issues, display more self-confidence, perform better academically and enjoy a better overall quality of life!

Tips from a former *Biggest Loser*

Jay Jacobs
Former contestant
of NBC's
The Biggest Loser

Jay Jacobs lost 181 pounds on Season 11 of NBC's *The Biggest Loser*.

Sedentary lifestyles, weight issues and unhealthy habits need to be addressed at home. It is more likely that your child will include healthy habits as part of their everyday life if they understand:

✔ Why staying active and eating healthy is important

✔ What are healthy habits and what are not

✔ How to be healthy, active and happy

Go to the Health and Wellness Index in the back of the book for more Family Health and Wellness Tips.

Warm Up!

It is always best to prepare your body for any physical activity by moving around and stretching.

Get Loose! Stretch!

Move your head from side to side, trying to touch each shoulder. Now move your head forward, touching your chin to your chest and then looking up and back as far as you can, trying to touch your back with the back of your head.

Touch your toes when standing, bend over at the waist and touch the end of your toes or the floor. Hold this for 10 seconds.

Get Moving

Walk or jog for 3-5 minutes to warm up before you exercise. Shake your arms and roll your shoulders when you are finished walking or jogging.

Healthy Eating and Nutrition

A healthy diet and daily exercise will maximize the likelihood of children growing up healthy and strong. Children are still growing and adding bone mass, so a balanced diet is very important to their overall health. Provide three nutritious meals a day that include fruits and vegetables. Try to limit fast food consumption, and find time to cook more at home where you know the source of your food and how your food is prepared. Provide your child with healthy, well-portioned snacks, and try to keep them from eating too much at a time.

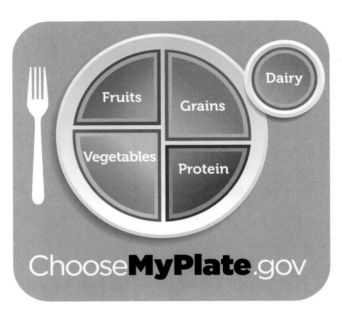

SCORE! A HEALTHY EATING GOAL

As a rule of thumb, avoid foods and drinks that are high in sugars, fat, or caffeine. Try to provide fruits, vegetables, grains, lean meats, chicken, fish, and low-fat dairy products as part of a healthy meal when possible. Obesity and being overweight, even in children, can significantly increase the risk of heart disease, diabetes, and other chronic illnesses. Creating an active lifestyle this summer that includes healthy eating and exercise will help your child maintain a healthy weight and protect them from certain illnesses throughout the year.

Let's Eat Healthy!

5 Steps to Improve Eating Habits of Your Family

1) Make fresh fruits and veggies readily available.
2) Cook more at home, and sit down for dinner as a family.
3) Limit consumption of soda, desserts and sugary cereals.
4) Serve smaller portions.
5) Limit snacks to just one or two daily.

Technology and Child Development

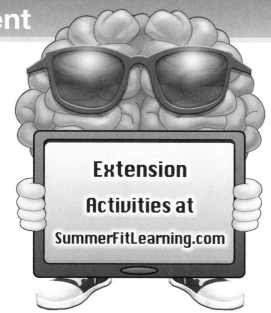

Children start developing initiative and creativity at a young age. Technology offers children additional outlets to learn and demonstrate their creativity. However, it is critical that active playtime and traditional learning resources including crayons, paint, books and toys are included as an essential part of the child's daily routine in addition to technology use. Used appropriately, computers can be a positive element of children's play and learning as they explore and experiment. Screen time (including TV, computer, phone and games) should be limited to a maximum of one to two hours per day for young children (American Academy of Pediatrics).

Extension Activities at SummerFitLearning.com

3 KEYS TO TECH SUCCESS

1 Consider technology as one tool among many used to enhance learning, not as a replacement for child interactions with each other, with adults, or other modes of learning.

2 Explore touch screens with a wide variety of appropriate interactive media experiences with your child. Verbally communicate with them the concepts of the game or apps that engage them. Express interest and encouragement of their performance.

3 Establish "No Screen Zones" for children such as the dinner table at home and in public settings. Screens create barriers that are difficult to talk through and can easily isolate children and parents. Establishing appropriate times and places to use technology will help children develop "tech-etiquette."

Core Values in the Home

Understanding core values allows your child to have a clearer understanding of their own behavior in your home, in their classroom and in our communities. Core values are fundamental to society and are incorporated into our civil laws, but are taught first and foremost at home. Parents and guardians are the most important and influential people in a child's life. It is up to you to raise children who respect and accept themselves, and others around them.

Role Models

A role model is a person who serves as an example of a particular value or trait. There are many people today, and throughout history, who exemplify in their own actions the values that we strive to have ourselves, and teach our children.

Mahatma Ghandi
Advocate for non-violence

RESPECT

Harriet Tubman
Civil Rights Activist

UNDERGROUND R.R.

TRUSTWORTHY

Bullying

In recent years, bullying has become a leading topic of concern. It is a complex issue, and can be difficult for parents to know what to do when they hear that their child is being bullied or is bullying others. Bullying is always wrong. It is critical that you intervene appropriately when bullying occurs. Make sure your child understands what bullying means. Check in with your child often to make sure he/she knows you are interested and aware of what is going on in their social lives.

Learn more at StopBullying.gov

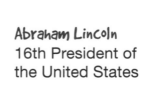

HONESTY

#1

Abraham Lincoln
16th President of the United States

Books Build Better Brains!

Reading is considered the gateway to all learning, so it is critical as a parent or caregiver to assist and encourage children to read at all grade levels regardless of reading ability.

1. Create a daily reading routine. A reading routine provides the practice a child needs to reinforce and build reading and literacy skills.

2. Create a summer reading list. Choose a variety of children's books, including fairy tales, poems, fiction and non-fiction books.

3. Join or start a summer reading club. Check your local public library or bookstore.

4. Talk with your child about a book that you are reading. Let your child see how much you enjoy reading and ask them to share stories from some of their favorite books.

5. Children love to hear stories about their family. Tell your child what it was like when you or your parents were growing up, or talk about a funny thing that happened when you were their age. Have them share stories of their own about when they were "young."

Read 20 minutes a day!

CYBER READERS: Books in a Digital World

With the amount of electronic resources available, children are gaining access to subjects faster than ever before. With electronic resources comes a significant amount of "screen time" that children spend with technology including television, movies, computers, phones and gaming systems. It is important to manage "screen time" and include time for books. Reading a book helps develop attention spans and allows children to build their imaginations without the aid of animated graphics, special effects and sound that may hinder a child's ability to create these for themselves.

The key to a good summer reading list is having a wide variety of books. Visit the library and let your child choose titles of their own and ask the librarian for recommendations.

Color the ⭐ for every title read and the **Book Report activity page** (in the back of the book) is completed. Go to SummerFitLearning.com to download and print out more **Book Report activity pages** to complete.

Fairy tales, folk tales, and nursery rhymes including: "Cinderella," "The Gingerbread Man," "Little Red Riding Hood," "The Three Little Pigs," "The Three Billy Goats Gruff," "Goldilocks and the Three Bears," and "Mother Goose Rhymes"

☆ **The Berenstain Bears**
Berenstain, Stan and Jan

☆ **Curious George**
Rey, H.A.

☆ **Clifford, the Big Red Dog**
Bridwell, Norman

☆ **Miss Nelson Is Missing!**
Allard, Harry

☆ **Goodnight, Moon**
Brown, Margaret W.

☆ **Draw Draw Draw**
Ames, Lee J

☆ **Make Way for Ducklings**
McCloskey, Robert

☆ **The Tale of Peter Rabbit**
Potter, Beatrix

☆ **Harry the Dirty Dog**
Zion, Gene

☆ **There's a Nightmare in My Closet**
Mayer, Mercer

☆ **Madeline**
Bemelmans, Ludwig

☆ **Where the Wild Things Are**
Sendak, Maurice

☆ **Caps for Sale**
Solbodkina, Esphyr

☆ **The Very Hungry Caterpillar**
Carle, Eric

☆ **The Cat in the Hat**
Seuss, Dr.

☆ **The Little Engine That Could**
Piper, Watty

☆ **Ira Sleeps Over**
Waber, Bernard

Preschool Skills Assessment

Parents, this assessment test is for you to do with your child to determine kindergarten readiness. It is an opportunity to pinpoint your child's strengths and weaknesses in order to determine where additional practice is needed. The first set of questions is for you to answer. The second set of questions is for you to do with your child.

Part 1

1. Can your child dress himself/herself? _____ Tie his/her shoes? _____

2. Can your child go to the bathroom by himself/herself? _____

3. Can your child listen to instructions and follow directions? _____

4. Does your child get along with other children? _____

5. Can your child hold a pencil correctly? _____

6. Can your child cut with scissors? _____

7. Does your child know the alphabet or at least be familiar with it? _____

8. Can your child count to 10? _____

9. Can your child hop? _____ Skip? _____ Jump? _____

10. Is your child able to identify and express his/her emotions? _____

11. Does your child speak in sentences? _____

12. Does your child try to read by telling a story based on pictures? _____

Part 2:

1. I can write my name. I can say the letters in my name.

_____ .

2. Trace the lines from left to right.

3. Copy the uppercase letters.

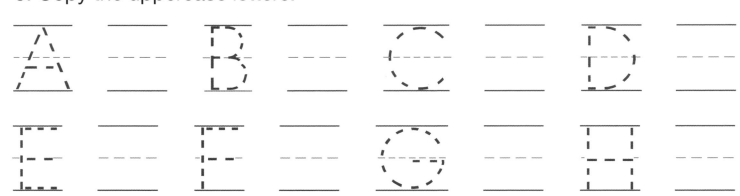

4. Copy the lowercase letters

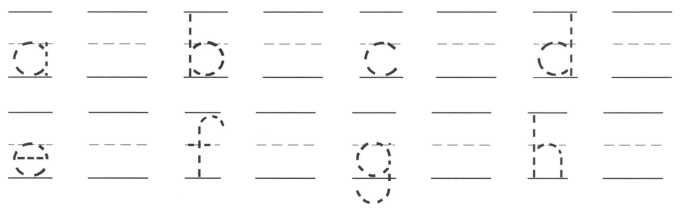

5. What does not belong in the group? Put an X on it.

6. Draw a happy face.	Draw a sad face.

7. Name the shapes.

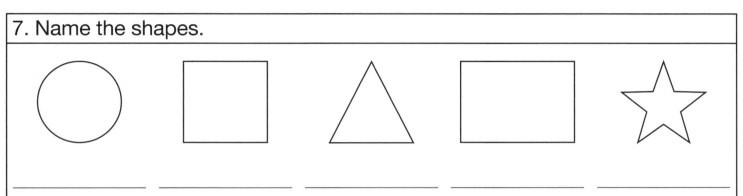

_____ _____ _____ _____ _____

8. Color the circle red.   Color the square blue.   Color the triangle green.

Color the rectangle orange.   Color the star yellow.

9. I can count to :_____

10. Trace the numbers. (in dotted lines)

11. Circle the plane that is up.

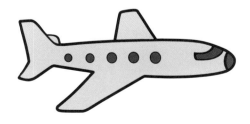

12. Circle the two pictures that are alike.

13. How many spiders?

_____

14. Circle the bigger mouse.

15. Circle the word that rhymes with cat.

16. What comes next?

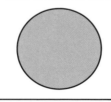 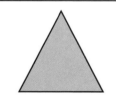 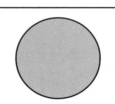 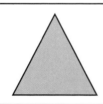 

17. Draw a line to match the pictures.

PARENT GUIDE WEEK 1

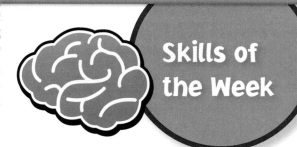

Skills of the Week

Honesty

Abraham Lincoln

- ✔ Color words
- ✔ The letter B
- ✔ The letter C
- ✔ Animal homes
- ✔ Write numbers 1-10
- ✔ Cardinal numbers
- ✔ Counting cents
- ✔ Shapes
- ✔ Finish the pattern
- ✔ Missing numbers

Honesty means being fair, truthful, and trustworthy. Honesty means telling the truth no matter what. People who are honest do not lie, cheat, or steal.

Sometimes it is not easy to tell the truth, especially when you are scared and do not want to get in trouble or let others down. Try to remember that even when it is difficult, telling the truth is always the best way to handle any situation, and people will respect you more.

Play Every Day!

Weekly Extension Activities at SummerFitLearning.com

Honesty In Action!
Color the star each day you show honesty through your own actions.

WEEK 1

HEALTHY MIND + HEALTHY BODY

Color the ⭐ As You Complete Your Daily Task

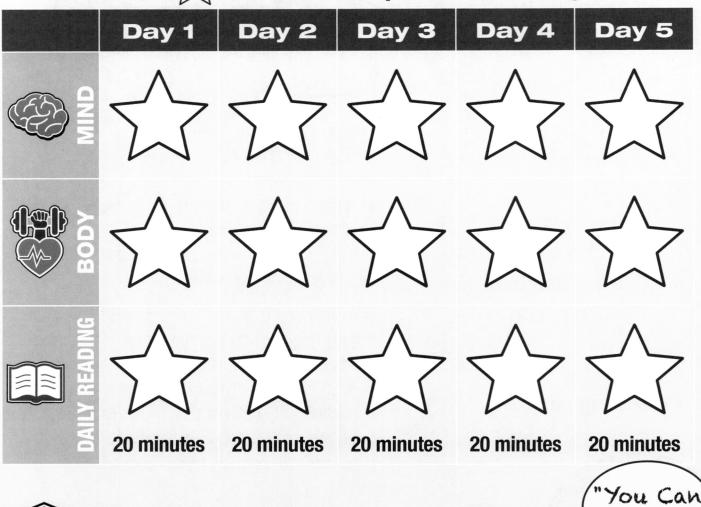

	Day 1	Day 2	Day 3	Day 4	Day 5
MIND	☆	☆	☆	☆	☆
BODY	☆	☆	☆	☆	☆
DAILY READING	☆ 20 minutes	☆ 20 minutes	☆ 20 minutes	☆ 20 minutes	☆ 20 minutes

"I am honest"

"You Can do It"

_____
Print Name

Letters and Sounds

A a

Ant starts with A a.

Trace and write the letter A a.

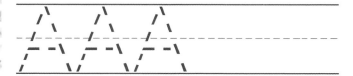

Circle the pictures that begin with the sound of A a.

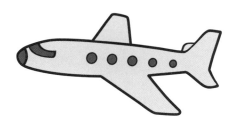

Aerobic
Go to www.summerfitlearning.com for more Activities!

Exercise for today
Tag
Color the star when you complete each level.

☆ **10-30 Seconds**
☆ **31-60 Seconds**
☆ **61-90 Seconds**

Be Healthy!
Eat an apple!

WEEK 1

Numbers and Math

How many alligators? _____

Learn Your Numbers - Trace and write the number 1

DAY 1

20 © Summer Fit

 **Honesty in Action**

"I am honest when I share and show my feelings."

Color the star if you shared your true feelings today.

B b

Bat starts with B b.

Trace and write the letter B b.

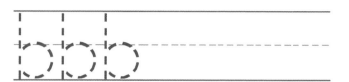

Circle the pictures that begin with the sound of B b.

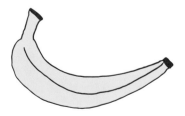

Exercise for today
Leg Scissors
Color the star when you complete each level.

☆ 1-5 Reps
☆ 6-10 Reps
☆ 10-20 Reps

Be Healthy!
Fresh fruits come from your garden or a farm.

WEEK 1

DAY 2

 Learn Your Letters - Trace and write the number 2

2 2 2

Numbers and Math - How many spots on the Ladybug?

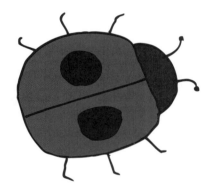

_____

Count the bugs and trace the number.

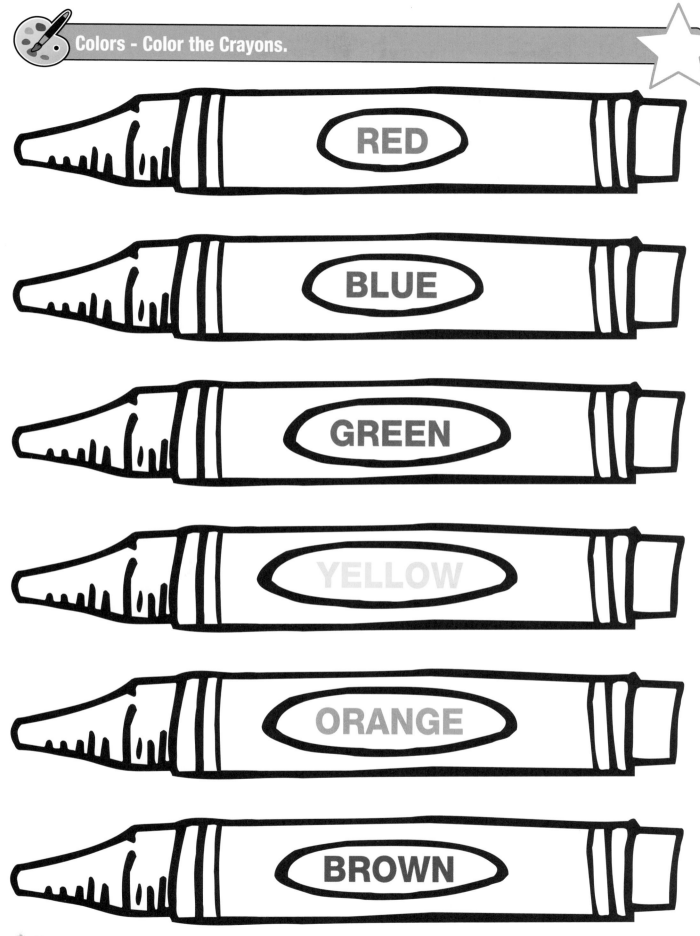

RED

BLUE

GREEN

YELLOW

ORANGE

BROWN

Aerobic

Go to www.summerfitlearning.com for more Activities!

Exercise for today
Foot Bag
Color the star when you complete each level.

☆ **10-30 Seconds**
☆ **31-60 Seconds**
☆ **61-90 Seconds**

Be Healthy!
Walnuts look like a brain- they make you smart!

WEEK 1

DAY 3

Shapes - Trace the shapes and draw your own

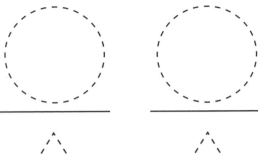

Shapes - Color the triangles red. Color the circles blue.

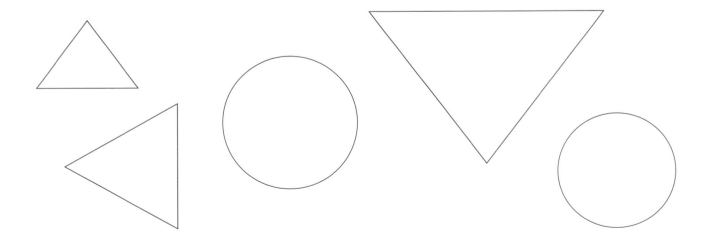

How many triangles did you color? _____

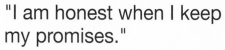 **Letters and Sounds**

 Honesty in Action

"I am honest when I keep my promises."

Color the star if you kept a promise today.

 **C c**

Cat begins with the letter C c.

Trace and write the letter C c.

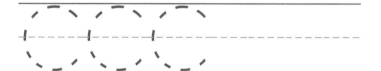

Circle the pictures that begin with the sound of C c.

Exercise for today
Ankle Touches

Color the star when you complete each level.

☆ **1-5 Reps**
☆ **6-10 Reps**
☆ **10-20 Reps**

Be Healthy!
Breakfast is very important!

WEEK 1

Numbers - Trace and write the number 3

3   3   3

Math - How many cats are on the wall?

DAY 4

Honesty means to tell the truth.

Abraham Lincoln

Abraham Lincoln was a president of the United States. People called him "Honest Abe" because he always told the truth.

Circle each picture that is true

"Believe in yourself!"

Choose 1 or more activities to do with your family or friends. Color today's star when you are finished. Good job!

☐ Play a game of hide and seek and no peaking!

☐ Make a mask of an animal you would like to pretend to be. Then, take it off and be who you really are.

☐ Learn this poem and make it into a song:

Tell the truth, tell the truth
Each and every day
Be honest and be truthful
In all you do and say

Core Value Book List
Read More About Honesty

The Empty Pot
By Demi

Sam Tells Stories
By Thierry Robberecht

The Emperors New Clothes
By Hans C. Anderson

Reading Extension Activities at SummerFitLearning.com

 Let's Talk About It

All preschoolers lie occasionally and often it is a result of very active imaginations. At this age it is important to distinguish what is real from what is make believe, what is true and what is not true. Play a game with your child saying things like "cows can fly". Let your child respond "true or not true." Remember children learn from example, so practice what you preach.

Play Time!
Choose a Game or Activity to Play for 60 minutes today!

YOU CHOOSE

_____
Write down which game or activity you played today!

 **Be Healthy!** Name a fruit or vegetable that is green.

Watch exercise videos at www.summerfitlearning.com

WEEK 2

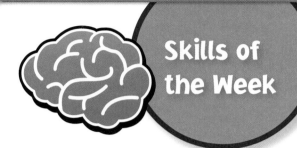

Skills of the Week

✔ The letter D
✔ The letter F
✔ Draw the word
✔ Beginning sounds
✔ Count back from 10
✔ Finish the shape
✔ Patterns
✔ Counting cents
✔ Addition

Compassion

Mother Teresa

Compassion is caring about the feelings and needs of others.

Sometimes we are so focused on our own feelings that we don't care how other people feel. If we consider other's feelings before our own the world can be a much kinder place. Take time to do something nice for another person and you will feel better about yourself.

GET FIT TIME!

Play Every Day!

Weekly Extension Activities at SummerFitLearning.com

Compassion In Action!
Color the star each day you show compassion through your own actions.

Color the ⭐ As You Complete Your Daily Task

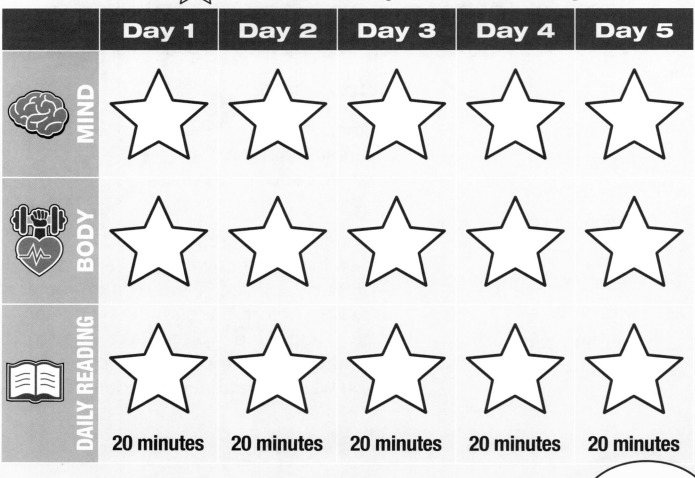

	Day 1	Day 2	Day 3	Day 4	Day 5
MIND	⭐	⭐	⭐	⭐	⭐
BODY	⭐	⭐	⭐	⭐	⭐
DAILY READING	⭐	⭐	⭐	⭐	⭐
	20 minutes	20 minutes	20 minutes	20 minutes	20 minutes

"I am compassionate"

"You Can do It"

_____

Print Name

Compassion in Action

"I am compassionate when I care about others."

Color the star if you showed someone compassion today.

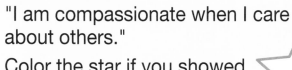

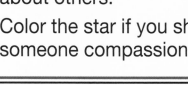

D d

Dog begins with the letter D d.

Trace and write the letter D d.

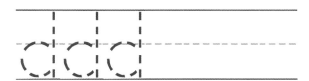

Circle the pictures that begin with the sound of D d.

WEEK 2

DAY 1

Aerobic

Go to www.summerfitlearning.com for more Activities!

Exercise for today
Tree Sprints
Color the star when you complete each level.

☆ **10-30 Seconds**
☆ 31-60 Seconds
☆ **61-90 Seconds**

Be Healthy!
Each color vegetable gives you a different power to be healthy!

WEEK 2

Math - Color the spots black

How many spots on the dog? _____

Numbers - Trace and write the number 4

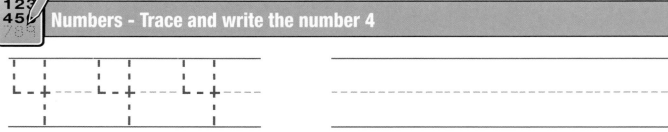

How many ducks?

2   4   3

How many dogs?

4   2   3

DAY 1

© Summer Fit

Compassion in Action

"I am compassionate when I am kind to people and animals."

Color the star if you were kind to people or animals today.

E e

Egg begins with the letter E e.

Trace and write the letter E e.

Circle the pictures that begin with the sound of E e.

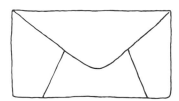

Exercise for today
Push-ups
Color the star when you complete each level.

☆ **1-5 Reps**
☆ **6-10 Reps**
☆ **10-20 Reps**

WEEK 2

Math - How many eggs are in the nest? Color the eggs blue.

How many? _____

Numbers - Trace and write the number 5

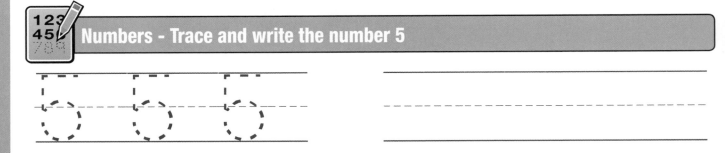

Draw an X on 5 bugs.

DAY 2

Self-Concept

Compassion in Action

"I am compassionate when I share."
Color the star if you shared with someone today.

You are special.
There is only 1 of you.

Write your name.

_____

- - - - - - - - - - - - - - - - - -

_____

I have _____ **eyes.   I have** _____ **hair.**

Draw a picture of yourself.

Exercise for today
Jumping Jacks
Color the star when you complete each level.

☆ **10-30 Seconds**
☆ **31-60 Seconds**
☆ **61-90 Seconds**

WEEK 2

DAY 3

Compare - Match each dog to the right size bone.

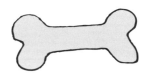

Circle the largest dog. Underline the smallest dog.

Compassion in Action

"I am compassionate when I help others."

Color the star if you helped someone today.

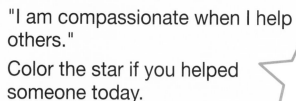

F f

Frog begins with the letter F f.

Trace and write the letter F f.

Circle the pictures that begin with the sound of F f.

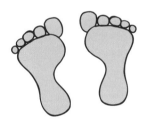  

WEEK 2

DAY 4

Strength

Go to www.summerfitlearning.com for more Activities!

Exercise for today
Moon Touches

Color the star when you complete each level.

☆ **1-5 Reps**
☆ **6-10 Reps**
☆ **10-20 Reps**

Be Healthy!
Cook a meal with your family today.

WEEK 2

Numbers - Trace and write the number 6.

6 6 6

Math - How many spiders are on the web?

_____

How many?

Circle the dog that is "in" the house.

DAY 4

Compassion is caring about others.

Mother Teresa

Mother Teresa helped many sick and poor people in India. She cared about everyone she met. Mother Teresa treated others the way she wanted to be treated.

Circle the picture of a friend showing compassion.

"Believe in yourself!"

Choose 1 or more activities to do with your family or friends. Color today's star when you are finished. Good job!

☐ Draw a picture for someone who is sick or sad.

☐ Share your toys with a younger brother or sister.

☐ Put out some birdseed or make a bird feeder for the birds in your neighborhood.

Spread peanut butter on a pinecone and roll in birdseed. Tie a piece of string around it and hang it in a tree.

Core Value Book List
Read More About Compassion

Horace and Morris But Mostly Dolores
By James Howe

Sumi's First Day of School
By Soyung Pak

Yoko
By Rosemary Wells

Reading Extension Activities at SummerFitLearning.com

Let's Talk About It

Model compassion and your kids will learn to be compassionate. Talk with your child about what others experience and how they might feel in a given situation. Ask them how it would feel to be in their shoes. For example, after seeing a homeless person, ask your child how they would feel if that was them.

Play Time!
Choose a Game or Activity to Play for 60 minutes today!

YOU CHOOSE

Write down which game or activity you played today!

Be Healthy! Wash your hands.

Watch exercise videos at www.summerfitlearning.com

WEEK 3

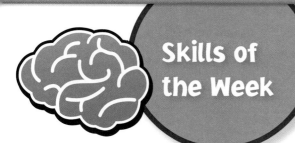

Skills of the Week

✔ The letter G
✔ The letter H
✔ Partner letters
✔ Short a
✔ Days of the week
✔ Missing numbers
✔ Time
✔ Finish the pattern
✔ Cardinal numbers
✔ Subtraction
✔ Graphing
✔ Counting backwards

Trustworthiness

Harriet Tubman

Trustworthiness is being worthy of trust. It means people can count on you.

You are honest and you keep your word. Sometimes it is easy to forget what we tell people because we try to do too much or we are constantly moving around. Try to slow down and follow through on what you say before moving onto something else.

Play Every Day!

Weekly Extension Activities at SummerFitLearning.com

Trust In Action!
Color the star each day you show trustworthiness through your own actions.

Color the ⭐ As You Complete Your Daily Task

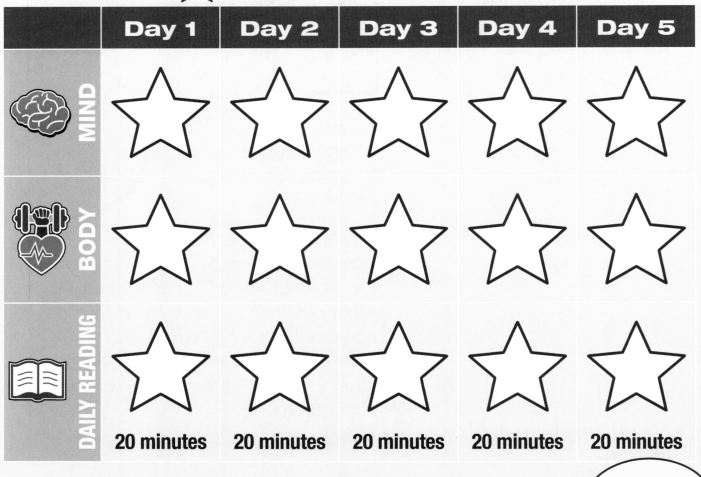

	Day 1	Day 2	Day 3	Day 4	Day 5
MIND	☆	☆	☆	☆	☆
BODY	☆	☆	☆	☆	☆
DAILY READING	☆	☆	☆	☆	☆
	20 minutes	20 minutes	20 minutes	20 minutes	20 minutes

"You Can do It"

"I am trustworthy"

_____
Print Name

Letters and Sounds

Trust in Action

"I am being trustworthy when I keep my promises."

Color the star if you kept a promise today.

G g

Guitar begins with the letter G g.

Trace and write the letter G g.

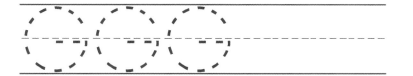

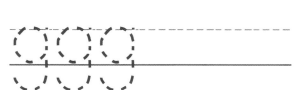

Circle the pictures that begin with the sound of G g.

WEEK 3

DAY 1

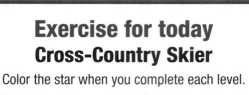

Aerobic Go to www.summerfitlearning.com for more Activities!

Exercise for today
Cross-Country Skier
Color the star when you complete each level.

☆ **10-30 Seconds**
☆ **31-60 Seconds**
☆ **61-90 Seconds**

Be Healthy!
Instead of juice, mix a piece of fruit with water.

WEEK 3

DAY 1

Numbers - Trace and write the number 7.

Circle 7 ants.

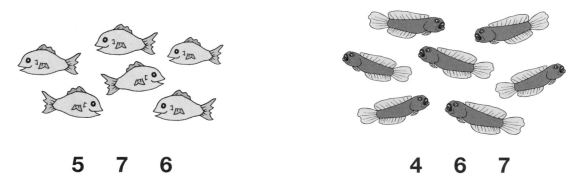

How many? Circle the correct number.

5   7   6   4   6   7

Circle the tallest flower.

H h

Hippopotamus begins with the letter H h.

Trace and write the letter H h.

Circle the pictures that begin with the sound of H h.

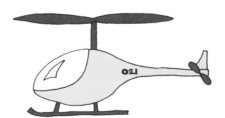

WEEK 3

DAY 2

Exercise for today
Chop and Squat
Color the star when you complete each level.

☆ **1-5 Reps**
☆ **6-10 Reps**
☆ **10-20 Reps**

Be Healthy!
Instead of a sweet, try toast with cream cheese or peanut butter!

WEEK 3

Art and numbers - Draw 8 legs on the spider's body.

Learn Your Numbers -

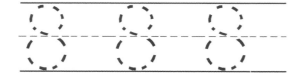

Circle the smallest hat.

DAY 2

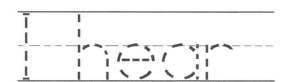 with my

 with my

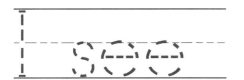 with my

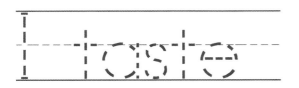 with my

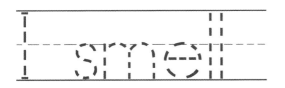 with my

 with my

Exercise for today
Hide and Seek
Color the star when you complete each level.

☆ **10-30 Seconds**
☆ 31-60 Seconds
☆ **61-90 Seconds**

Be Healthy!
Instead of potato chips, try POPCORN!

Shapes and sizes - Circle the one that is taller

Circle the longest worm.

Circle the shortest pencil.

How many pennies?

WEEK 3

DAY 3

Trust in Action

"I am being trustworthy when I do the right thing."

Color the star if you did the right thing today.

I i

Ice Cream begins with the letter I i.

Trace and write the letter I i.

Circle the pictures of things that begin with I i.

Strength Go to www.summerfitlearning.com for more Activities!

Exercise for today
Fly in the Ointment
Color the star when you complete each level.

☆ 1-5 Reps
☆ 6-10 Reps
☆ 10-20 Reps

Be Healthy!
Take a walk with your parents today.

Numbers and Math - Color 9 of the snails.

Numbers - Trace and write the number 9

Color the largest star yellow. Color the smallest star blue.

WEEK 3

DAY 4

Being Trustworthy means keeping your promises.

Harriet Tubman

Harriet Tubman helped many slaves escape and be free. People trusted her with their lives and she never let them down. Even though what she was doing was dangerous, Harriet kept her word and helped the people she said she would.

When I make a promise I keep my word, I am trustworthy.

Mom said I may have 2 cookies, color how many cookies I should take.

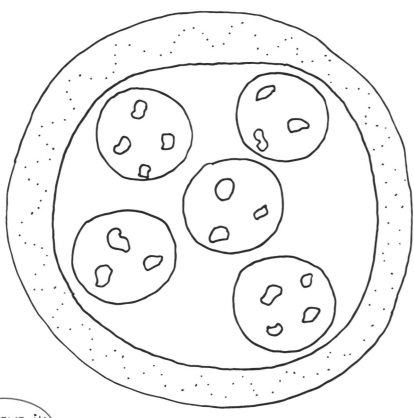

"Believe in yourself!"

Choose 1 or more activities to do with your family or friends. Color today's star when you are finished. Good job!

☐ **Practice keeping your word.** When your parents ask you to do something, do it right away.

☐ Our pets trust us to take care of them. Be trustworthy and give your pet food and water every day.

☐ Being trustworthy means you follow the rules. With your parent make a list of all the family rules. Talk about what happens when you follow the rules and what happens when you don't.

Core Value Book List
Read More About Trustworthy

Tales of Peter Rabbit
By Beatrix Potter

The Apple and the Arrow
By Mary and Conrad Buff

The Boy Who Cried Wolf
Retold by Katherine Evans

Reading Extension Activities at SummerFitLearning.com

Let's Talk About It

Discuss why telling the truth is important at all times. Be consistent at home with rules and consequences and only make promises you intend to keep. Tell the truth to your child and tell the truth in front of your child.

Stepping Stones

Stepping Stones Entertainment™ was founded by parents who wanted to provide meaningful family movies to help inspire common values. It is made up of people from many different backgrounds, nationalities and beliefs. For more than 20 years, Stepping Stones has provided families with movies about integrity, charity, forgiveness and many other common values through hundreds of films for all ages. Learn more at **www.steppingstones.com**.

STEPPING STONES.com
Meaningful Family Movies

Play Time!
Choose a Game or Activity to Play for 60 minutes today!

YOU CHOOSE

_____

Write down which game or activity you played today!

Be Healthy!
Plant a family garden and eat what you grow.

Watch exercise videos at www.summerfitlearning.com

WEEK 4

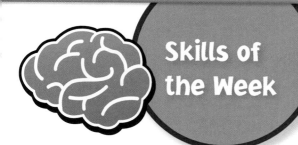

Skills of the Week

- ✔ The letter I
- ✔ The letter J
- ✔ The letter K
- ✔ Beginning sounds
- ✔ The letter L
- ✔ Short e
- ✔ Connect the dots
- ✔ Subtraction
- ✔ Counting dimes
- ✔ Draw the gum balls
- ✔ Addition
- ✔ Subtraction.

Self-Discipline

Stephanie Lopez Cox

Self-discipline means self-control. It is working hard and getting yourself to do what is important.

It is easy to lose interest in what you are doing, especially if it does not come fast and easy. Focus your attention on what you are trying to accomplish and try to block out other things until you reach your goal.

GET FIT TIME!

Play Every Day!

Weekly Extension Activities at SummerFitLearning.com

Self-Discipline In Action!
Color the star each day you show self-discipline through your own actions.

WEEK 4

Color the ⭐ As You Complete Your Daily Task

	Day 1	Day 2	Day 3	Day 4	Day 5
MIND	⭐	⭐	⭐	⭐	⭐
BODY	⭐	⭐	⭐	⭐	⭐
DAILY READING	⭐ 20 minutes	⭐ 20 minutes	⭐ 20 minutes	⭐ 20 minutes	⭐ 20 minutes

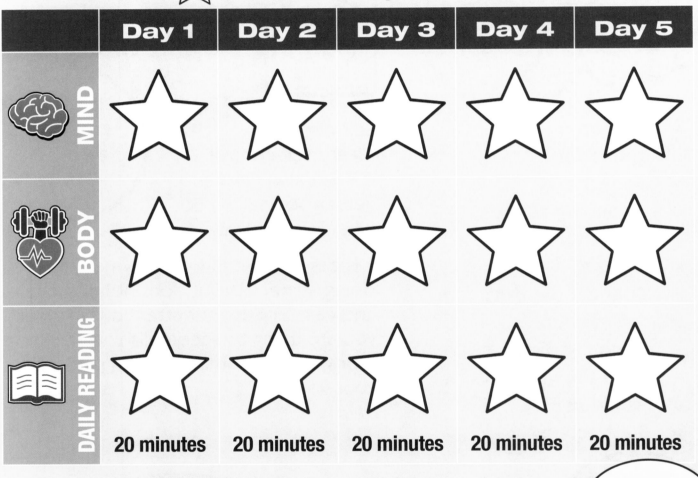

"You Can do It"

"I am self-disciplined"

_____
Print Name

Self-discipline in Action

"I practice self-discipline when I am in control of my actions."

Color the star if you had self-discipline today.

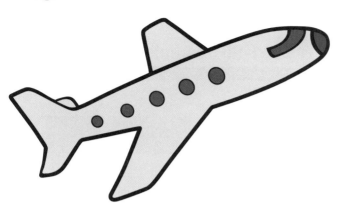

J j

Jet begins with the letter J j.

Trace and write the letter J j.

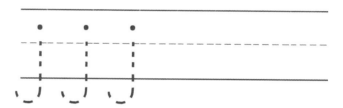

Circle the pictures that begin with the sound of J j.

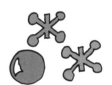

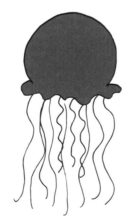

WEEK 4

DAY 1

Aerobic Go to www.summerfitlearning.com for more Activities!

Exercise for today
Turtle and Rabbit
Color the star when you complete each level.

☆ **10-30 Seconds**
☆ 31-60 Seconds
☆ **61-90 Seconds**

Be Healthy!
Try a new food today.

Numbers and Math - Count the fingers.

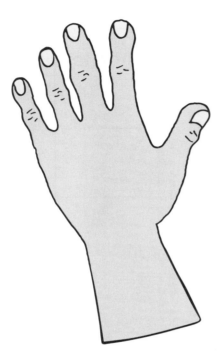
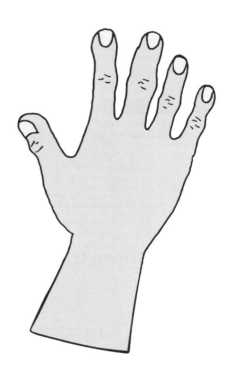

Draw a watch on the left hand. Draw a ring on the right hand.

Numbers - Trace and write the number 10.

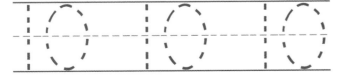

Self-discipline in Action

"I practice self-discipline when I am in control of my actions."

Color the star if you had self-discipline today.

K k

Kangaroo begins with the letter K k.

Color the kangaroo blue.

Trace and write the letter K k.

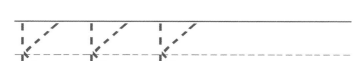

Color the pictures that begin with the sound of K k.

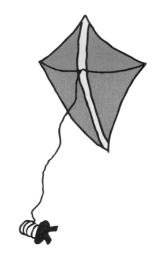

WEEK 4

DAY 2

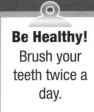

Exercise for today
Jumping Jacks
Color the star when you complete each level.

☆ 1-5 Reps
☆ 6-10 Reps
☆ 10-20 Reps

WEEK 4

Numbers and Math - Trace the number and the number word.

Draw the number of flowers in each pot.

One

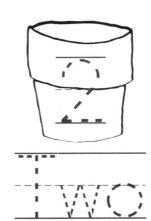

Two

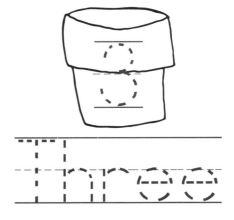

Three

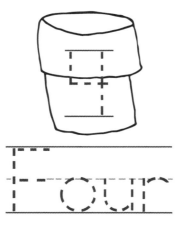

Four

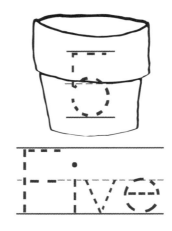

Five

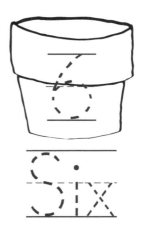

Six

DAY 2

Circle the pictures of healthy food.

WEEK 4

DAY 3

© Summer Fit

59

Aerobic
Go to www.summerfitlearning.com for more Activities!

Exercise for today
Wheel Over

Color the star when you complete each level.

☆ **10-30 Seconds**
☆ 31-60 Seconds
☆ **61-90 Seconds**

Be Healthy!
Eat your snack at the table, not in front of the computer or television.

WEEK 4

DAY 3

Matching - Draw a line to match the things that go together.

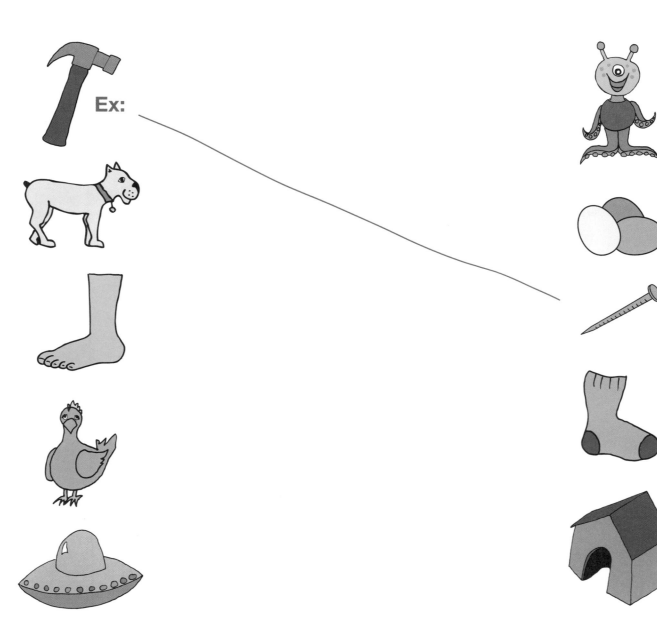

Ex:

Self-discipline in Action

"I practice self-discipline when I am in control of my actions."

Color the star if you had self-discipline today.

L l

Lion begins with the letter L l.

Trace and write the letter L l.

Circle the pictures that begin with the sound of L l.

Exercise for today
Jump Rope
Color the star when you complete each level.

☆ **1-5 Reps**
☆ 6-10 Reps
☆ **10-20 Reps**

Be Healthy!
Farmer's Market sells local produce.

Numbers and Math - Count from 1 to 10, connect the dots and color the turtle.

WEEK 4

DAY 4

Self-discipline is to have control of your actions.

Stephanie Lopez Cox is a great soccer player. Her hard work and self-discipline helped her get on the US National Soccer Team and win a gold medal in the Olympics. Stephanie practices very hard even when she doesn't feel like it and works hard to be the best athlete she can be.

Photo courtesy of Stephanie Lopez Cox

Do the right thing even when no one is watching.

Mom told Michael to clean up his toys before playing outside. Circle the picture of Michael practicing self-discipline.

"Believe in yourself!"

Choose 1 or more activities to do with your family or friends. Color today's star when you are finished. Good job!

☐ Talk with your parent about 3 things you can do to stay calm when you are angry such as: count to 10, scream into a pillow, or rip newspaper. Practice self-discipline in staying calm.

☐ Learn how to play a new game like checkers or chess. Practice self-discipline as you do your best to learn the rules.

☐ Make a chore chart with your parents. Earn a sticker for each job well done.

Core Value Book List
Read More About Self-Discipline

Mother, Mother, I Want Another
By Maria Polushkin

The Very Quiet Cricket
By Eric Carle

Gregory the Terrible Eater
By Mitchell Sharmat

Reading Extension Activities at SummerFitLearning.com

Let's Talk About It

Help your child learn to do the right thing because they want to not because they have to. Talk about different opportunities they have to show self-discipline at home and with their friends such as: cleaning up their toys, washing their hands, keeping their hands to themselves, eating healthy food, and expressing their feelings without yelling and screaming.

Play Time!
Choose a Game or Activity to Play for 60 minutes today!

YOU CHOOSE

_____
Write down which game or activity you played today!

Be Healthy!
Turn off the TV when you eat.

Watch exercise videos at www.summerfitlearning.com

PARENT GUIDE WEEK 5

Skills of the Week

- ✓ The letter M
- ✓ The four seasons
- ✓ The letter N
- ✓ The letter P
- ✓ How many in a dozen
- ✓ Smallest
- ✓ Biggest
- ✓ Number words
- ✓ Money
- ✓ Measurement
- ✓ Addition.

Kindness

Princess Diana

Kindness is caring about people, animals and the earth. It is looking for ways to help others.

Being nice to others catches on. When people are nice to each other they feel better about themselves and others. Small things make a big difference so when you smile, lend a helping hand and show concern for others, you are making the world a better place.

Play Every Day!

Weekly Extension Activities at SummerFitLearning.com

Kindness In Action!
Color the star each day you show kindness through your own actions.

WEEK 5

Color the ⭐ As You Complete Your Daily Task

	Day 1	Day 2	Day 3	Day 4	Day 5
MIND	☆	☆	☆	☆	☆
BODY	☆	☆	☆	☆	☆
DAILY READING	☆ 20 minutes	☆ 20 minutes	☆ 20 minutes	☆ 20 minutes	☆ 20 minutes

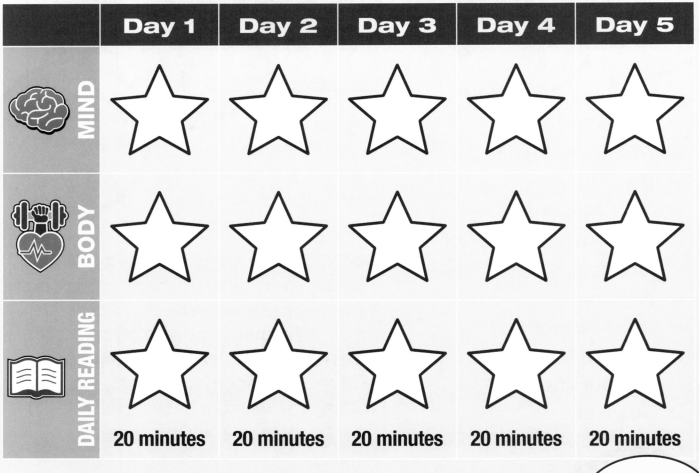

"I am kind"

"You Can do It"

_____

Print Name

Letters and Sounds

Kindness in Action

"I am kind when I share."
Color the star if you shared something today.

M m

Monkey begins with the letter M m.

Trace and write the letter M m.

Circle the pictures that begin with the sound of M m.

WEEK 5

DAY 1

67

Exercise for today
Dancing Shoes
Color the star when you complete each level.

☆ **10-30 Seconds**
☆ **31-60 Seconds**
☆ **61-90 Seconds**

Be Healthy!
Tell your family what made you feel happy today.

WEEK 5

Patterns - Color the patterns.

   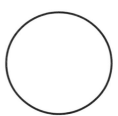 

 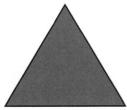  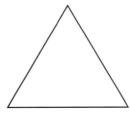 

 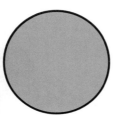  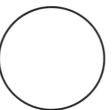 

DAY 1

Kindness in Action

"I am kind when I help."
Color the star if you helped someone today.

N n

Nuts begins with the letter N n.

Trace and write the letter N n.

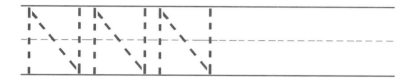

Circle the pictures that begin with the letter N n.

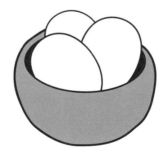

Exercise for today
Bear Crawl
Color the star when you complete each level.

☆ **1-5 Reps**
☆ **6-10 Reps**
☆ **10-20 Reps**

WEEK 5

Numbers and Math - Counting Coins

Count the pennies in the piggy banks. Circle the bank with the most pennies.

_____

_____

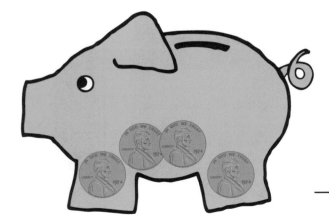

_____

DAY 2

Kindness in Action

"I am kind when I smile."
Color the star if you smiled at someone today.

O o

Octopus begins with the letter O o.

Trace and write the letter O o.

Circle the pictures that begin with the sound of O o.

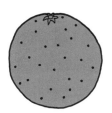

WEEK 5

DAY 3

Aerobic

Exercise for today
Run or Jog
Color the star when you complete each level.

☆ **10-30 Seconds**
☆ 31-60 Seconds
☆ **61-90 Seconds**

Be Healthy!
Quench your thirst with water or milk.

WEEK 5

DAY 3

Following directions - Circle the correct picture.

The mouse is "IN" the cup.

The cat is "UNDER" the table.

The bird is "OUT" of the nest.

Draw a worm on top of the apple. Color the apple red.

Kindness in Action

"I am kind when I share."
Color the star if you shared something today.

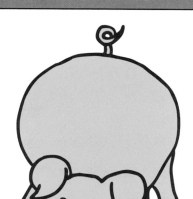

P p

Pig begins with the letter P p.

Trace and write the letter P p.

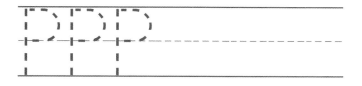

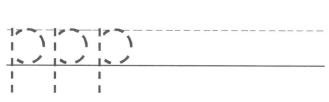

Circle the pictures that begin with the sound of P p.

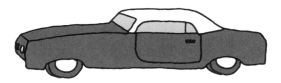

WEEK 5

DAY 4

Exercise for today
Hula-Hoop
Color the star when you complete each level.

☆ 1-5 Reps
☆ 6-10 Reps
☆ 10-20 Reps

WEEK 5

Numbers and Math - Pairs

A pair means 2 of something. Circle each pair.

DAY 4

Numbers - Trace and write the number 11.

I I I I I
I I I I I

© Summer Fit

Kindness is being nice and caring about people, animals, and the earth.

Princess Diana

Princess Diana was a kind princess who cared about others. She made everyone feel special no matter who they were. Princess Diana especially liked to visit sick children. She traveled around the world to share kind words and her smile.

There are many ways I can be kind.

Color the hearts that tell ways I can show kindness.

Put away my toys

"Kindness makes my heart glow"

Share my toys

Help set the table

Give a friend a hug

Smile at someone today

Hold the door open

"Believe in yourself!"

Choose 1 or more activities to do with your family or friends. Color today's star when you are finished. Good job!

☐ Put a sticker on your child each time you see him/her do something kind.

☐ Make a friendship bracelet out of beads and pipe cleaners to give to a friend.

☐ Make a Kindness tree out of construction paper and hang it up. Trace your child's hands on colorful paper and cut them out. Write on each hand something your child can do to show kindness. Hang them on the tree and each day let your child pick one to do.

Core Value Book List
Read More About Kindness

Alfie Lends a Hand
By Shirley Hughes

The Giving Tree
By Shel Silverstein

The Giant Hug
By Sandra Horning

Reading Extension Activities at SummerFitLearning.com

Let's Talk About It

Talk with your child about ways to show kindness. Ask them questions like "What can you say to someone who is sad?" Point out people you see being kind and explain to your child "Random Acts of Kindness." Plan as a family some ways you can do RAK every day.

Play Time!
Choose a Game or Activity to Play for 60 minutes today!

YOU CHOOSE

_____

Write down which game or activity you played today!

Be Healthy!
Have fruit with breakfast.

Watch exercise videos at www.summerfitlearning.com

WEEK 6

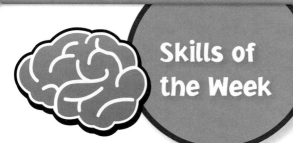

Skills of the Week

- ✔ The letter Q
- ✔ Beginning sounds
- ✔ The letter R
- ✔ Rhyming words
- ✔ What happens next
- ✔ Partner letters
- ✔ Subtraction
- ✔ Number sets
- ✔ Count by 10's
- ✔ Missing numbers
- ✔ Time
- ✔ Place value
- ✔ Finish the pattern
- ✔ Size comparison
- ✔ Location
- ✔ Addition

Courage

Rosa Parks

Courage means doing the right thing even when it is difficult and you are afraid. It means to be brave.

It can be a lot easier to do the right thing when everybody else is doing it, but it can be a lot harder to do it on our own or when nobody is looking. Remember who you are and stand up for what you believe in when it is easy and even more so when it is hard.

Play Every Day!

Weekly Extension Activities at SummerFitLearning.com

Courage In Action!
Color the star each day you show Courage through your own actions.

77

WEEK 6

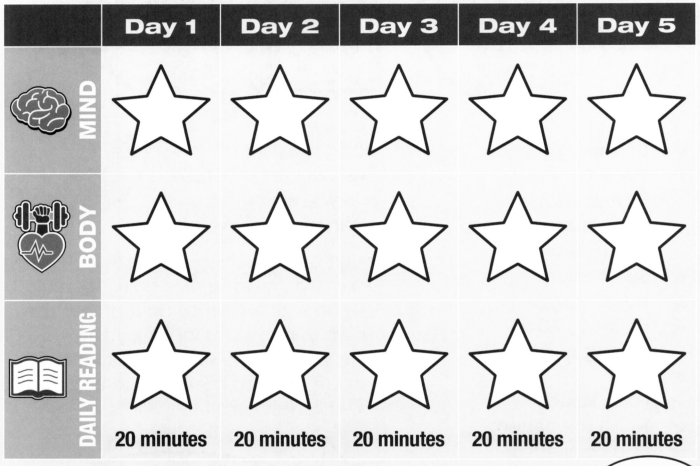

HEALTHY MIND + HEALTHY BODY

Color the ⭐ As You Complete Your Daily Task

	Day 1	Day 2	Day 3	Day 4	Day 5
MIND	☆	☆	☆	☆	☆
BODY	☆	☆	☆	☆	☆
DAILY READING	☆ 20 minutes	☆ 20 minutes	☆ 20 minutes	☆ 20 minutes	☆ 20 minutes

"I am brave"

"You Can do It"

Print Name

Courage in Action

"I am brave when I stand up for what is right."

Color the star if you showed courage today.

Q q

Queen begins with the letter Q q.

Trace and write the letter Q q.

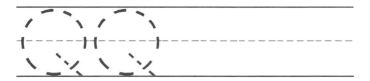

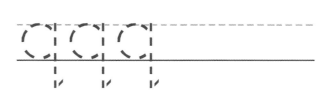

Circle the pictures that begin with the sound of Q q.

Exercise for today
Ghost Run or Jog
Color the star when you complete each level.

☆ **10-30 Seconds**
☆ 31-60 Seconds
☆ **61-90 Seconds**

Be Healthy!
Eat an apple!

 Math - 12 is a DOZEN of something.

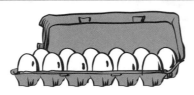 A dozen eggs is 12 eggs.

Circle a DOZEN donuts.

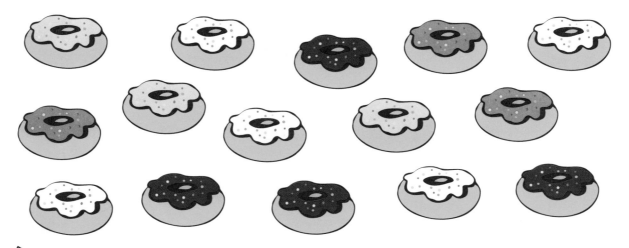

 **Learn Your Numbers - Trace and write the number 12**

Circle the purse with the most coins.

Courage in Action

"I am showing courage when I tell the truth."

Color the star if you told the truth all day today.

R r

Rainbow begins with the letter R r.

Trace and write the letter R r.

Circle the pictures that begin with the sound of R r.

WEEK 6

DAY 2

Strength

Go to www.summerfitlearning.com for more Activities!

Exercise for today
Crab Crawl
Color the star when you complete each level.

☆ **1-5 Reps**
☆ **6-10 Reps**
☆ **10-20 Reps**

Be Healthy!
Fresh fruits come from your garden or a farm.

🕐 **Time and Numbers - Trace the numbers on the clock.**

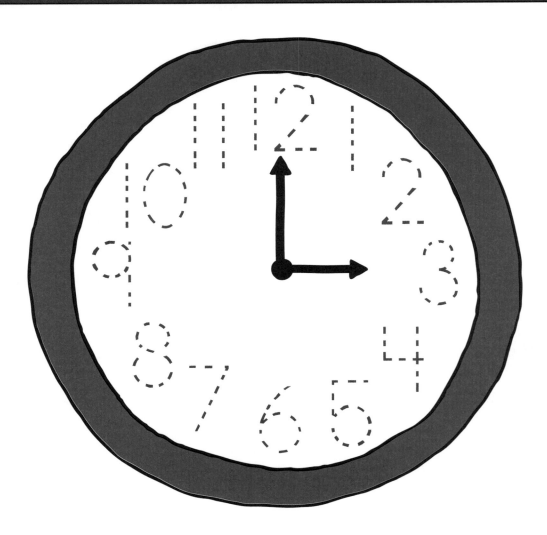

The big hand is on the _____ The little hand is on the _____

It is _____ o'clock.

It is my birthday. I feel...

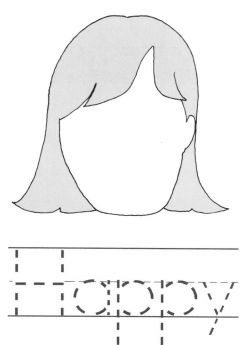

Happy

I fell off my bike. I feel...

Sad

I had a bad dream. I feel...

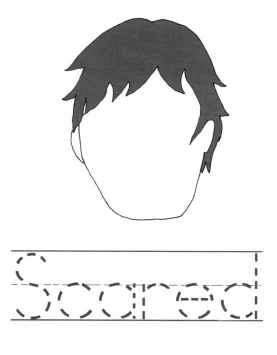

Scared

My friend took my toy. I feel..

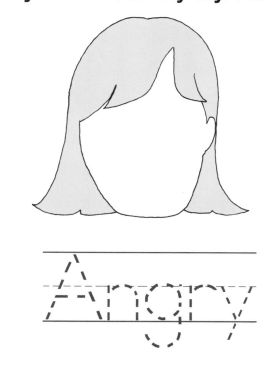

Angry

WEEK 6

DAY 3

Aerobic
Go to www.summerfitlearning.com for more Activities!

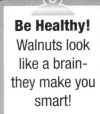

Exercise for today
Ball/Frisbee Toss and Run
Color the star when you complete each level.

☆ 10-30 Seconds
☆ 31-60 Seconds
☆ 61-90 Seconds

Be Healthy!
Walnuts look like a brain- they make you smart!

WEEK 6

DAY 3

 Sequencing - First, Next, Last.

Write 1 for what comes first, 2 for what comes next, and 3 for what comes last.

_____   _____   _____

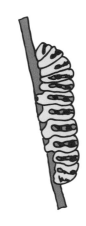

_____   _____   _____

Courage in Action

"I am showing courage when I try new things."

Color the star if you tried something new today.

S s

Sun begins with the letter S s.

Trace and write the letter S s.

Circle the pictures that begin with the sound of S s.

WEEK 6

DAY 4

Strength

Go to www.summerfitlearning.com for more Activities!

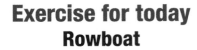

Exercise for today
Rowboat
Color the star when you complete each level.

☆ 1-5 Reps
☆ 6-10 Reps
☆ 10-20 Reps

WEEK 6

DAY 4

 Numbers and Math - How many? Trace the numbers.

How many...

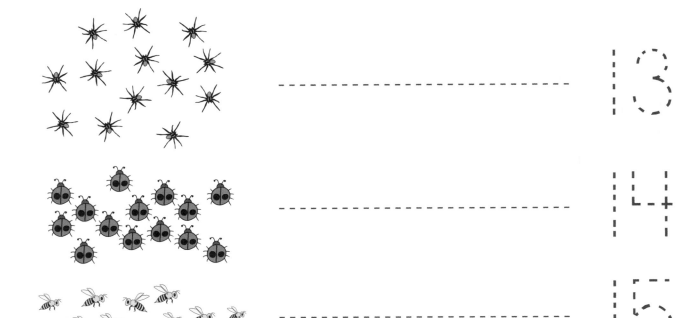

Finish the patterns:

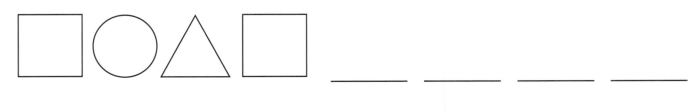

Courage means doing the right thing even when you are feeling scared.

Rosa Parks

Rosa Parks was brave. She showed great courage when she stood up for herself. Rosa Parks was asked to give up her seat because of the color of her skin. Rosa showed great courage when she did not give up her seat. She thought all people should be treated equally no matter what they looked like. Even though she was scared, she showed great courage and stood up for herself.

Circle the picture of Pablo showing courage.

Pablo is learning to ride his bike without training wheels. He is afraid of falling but has decided to be brave.

"Believe in yourself!"

Choose 1 or more activities to do with your family or friends. Color today's star when you are finished. Good job!

☐ Try a new food you think you won't like. You might be surprised.

☐ Try a new sport or activity.

☐ Draw a picture of something you are afraid of. Talk with your parents about how you can face your fear.

Core Value Book List
Read More About Courage

I'm Gonna Like Me
By Jamie Lee Curtis

The Little Engine That Could
By Watty Piper

The Wildest Brother
By Cornelia Funke

Reading Extension Activities at SummerFitLearning.com

Let's Talk About It

Remind your child that having courage does not mean that they are never scared but rather that they are able to face their fears. Discuss ways your child can show courage for example telling the truth, standing up for their friends, trying new things, and facing their fears. Catch your child being brave and praise them for their courage.

Play Time!
Choose a Game or Activity to Play for 60 minutes today!

YOU CHOOSE

_____

Write down which game or activity you played today!

Be Healthy!
Name a fruit or vegetable that is green.

Watch exercise videos at www.summerfitlearning.com

WEEK 7

Skills of the Week

✔ The letter S
✔ The letter T
✔ Opposites
✔ The letter V
✔ Matching letters
✔ Shapes
✔ Left
✔ Right
✔ Counting
✔ Addition
✔ Subtraction
✔ Following directions
✔ Money
✔ Time
✔ Count by 5's
✔ Calendars

Respect

Mahatma Gandhi

Respect is honoring yourself and others. It is behaving in a way that makes life peaceful and orderly.

Sometimes we forget to appreciate that every person is unique and different. All of us want to be accepted and appreciated for who we are. Try to treat others the way that you want to be treated, even when it is difficult.

Play Every Day!

GET FIT TIME!

Weekly Extension Activities at SummerFitLearning.com

Respect In Action!
Color the star each day you show respect through your own actions.

WEEK 7

HEALTHY MIND + HEALTHY BODY

Color the ⭐ As You Complete Your Daily Task

	Day 1	Day 2	Day 3	Day 4	Day 5
MIND	⭐	⭐	⭐	⭐	⭐
BODY	⭐	⭐	⭐	⭐	⭐
DAILY READING	⭐ 20 minutes	⭐ 20 minutes	⭐ 20 minutes	⭐ 20 minutes	⭐ 20 minutes

"I am respectful"

"You Can do It"

_____
Print Name

T t

Turtle begins with the letter T t.

Trace and write the letter T t.

Circle the pictures that begin with the sound of T t.

WEEK 7

DAY 1

Aerobic

Go to www.summerfitlearning.com for more Activities!

Exercise for today
Freeze Tag
Color the star when you complete each level.

☆ **10-30 Seconds**
☆ 31-60 Seconds
☆ 61-90 Seconds

Be Healthy!
Each color vegetable gives you a different power to be healthy!

WEEK 7

DAY 1

Shapes

A pentagon has 5 sides. A square has 4 sides. Color the pentagons blue. Color the squares red.

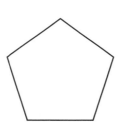  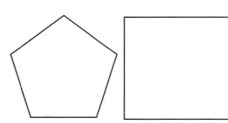

How many pentagons ? _____

How many squares ◼ ? _____

Respect in Action

"I show respect when I don't make fun of people."

Color the star if you did not make fun of anyone today.

U u

Ukulele begins with the letter U u.

Trace and write the letter U u.

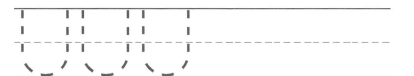

Circle the pictures that begin with the sound of U u.

DAY 2

Exercise for today
Freeze Dance
Color the star when you complete each level.

☆ **1-5 Reps**
☆ **6-10 Reps**
☆ **10-20 Reps**

Be Healthy!
Fresh vegetables come from your garden or a farm.

WEEK 7

DAY 2

Numbers and Math - Count the animals in the zoo.

How many elephants? _____

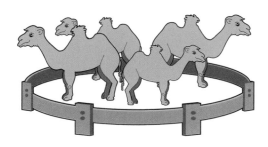

How many camels? _____

How many rhinoceros? _____

How many penguins? _____

How many giraffes? _____

How many ostrich? _____

"I show respect when I have good manners."

Color the star if you had good manners all day today.

V v

Violin begins with the letter V v.

Trace and write the letter V v.

Circle the pictures that begin with the sound of V v.

WEEK 7

DAY 3

Aerobic

Go to www.summerfitlearning.com for more Activities!

Exercise for today
Egg Race
Color the star when you complete each level.

☆ 10-30 Seconds
☆ 31-60 Seconds
☆ 61-90 Seconds

Be Healthy!
Make popsicles out of your favorite fruit juice!

1+2=3
Numbers and Math - Count the mice and circle how many.

3   5   7

2   4   6

7   8   9

3   4   5

Fill in the missing numbers.

1, _____, 3, 4, _____, 6, 7, _____, 9, 10.

© Summer Fit

Respect in Action

"I show respect when I am kind."
Color the star if you showed respect by being kind today.

W w

Wagon begins with the letter W w.

Trace and write the letter W w.

Circle the pictures that begin with the sound of W w.

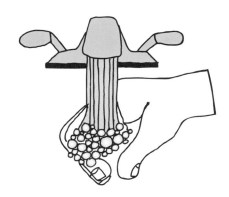

Strength

Go to www.summerfitlearning.com for more Activities!

Exercise for today
Snake Curl

Color the star when you complete each level.

☆ **1-5 Reps**
☆ 6-10 Reps
☆ **10-20 Reps**

Compare and Order - Cross off the one that doesn't belong in each row.

© Summer Fit

Respect is being nice to yourself and to others.

Mahatma Gandhi

Mahatma Gandhi was a great world leader. Gandhi taught people that when you hurt others you are hurting yourself. He wanted people to get along and not fight. He believed that if people would love and respect each other and each other's differences, there would be peace in the world.

No two people are exactly alike.

We all have differences that make us special and unique. Draw a picture of yourself and two friends. What things are the same? What things are different?

"Believe in yourself!"

Choose 1 or more activities to do with your family or friends. Color today's star when you are finished. Good job!

☐ Make a poster about yourself. Write on the top "I am a superstar!" Add pictures of yourself and have a parent write about all the things that make you special.

☐ Get a box of crayons and paper. Make a picture of a rainbow and color it with one color. Now look at the box of crayons. How much nicer would the rainbow be if it were colored using many colors? Now color another rainbow using many colors. Think about how boring the world would be if we were all the same. Our many differences bring color to the world.

Core Value Book List
Read More About Respect

The Sneetches and Other Stories
By Dr. Suess

We're Different, We're the Same
By Bobbi Kates

The Color of Us
By Karen Katz

Reading Extension Activities at SummerFitLearning.com

Children must develop self-respect in order for them to respect others. Respect is more than just having good manners; it must come from a core belief that others have as much worth as you. We must remind our children that it is not ok to hurt others or their property and to encourage a tolerance of others and their differences.

Play Time!
Choose a Game or Activity to Play for 60 minutes today!

YOU CHOOSE

Write down which game or activity you played today!

Be Healthy! Wash your hands.

Watch exercise videos at www.summerfitlearning.com

WEEK 8

Skills of the Week

- ✔ The letter W
- ✔ The letter X
- ✔ The letter Y
- ✔ The letter Z
- ✔ Beginning sounds
- ✔ Partner letters
- ✔ Following directions
- ✔ Pairs
- ✔ Addition
- ✔ Counting
- ✔ Finish the pattern
- ✔ Before and after
- ✔ Shapes
- ✔ Time
- ✔ Counting backwards by 10's

Responsibility

Terry Fox

Being responsible means others can depend on you. It is being accountable for what you do and for what you do not do.

A lot of times it is easier to look to someone else to step forward and do the work or to blame others when it does not get done. You are smart, capable and able so try to be the person who accepts challenges and does not blame others if it does not get done.

Play Every Day!

Weekly Extension Activities at SummerFitLearning.com

Responsibility In Action!

Color the star each day you show responsibility through your own actions.

WEEK 8

Color the ⭐ As You Complete Your Daily Task

		Day 1	Day 2	Day 3	Day 4	Day 5
🧠	MIND	⭐	⭐	⭐	⭐	⭐
💪	BODY	⭐	⭐	⭐	⭐	⭐
📖	DAILY READING	⭐	⭐	⭐	⭐	⭐
		20 minutes	20 minutes	20 minutes	20 minutes	20 minutes

"You Can do It"

"I am responsible"

_____

Print Name

"I am responsible when I keep my promises."

Color the star if you have kept your promises today.

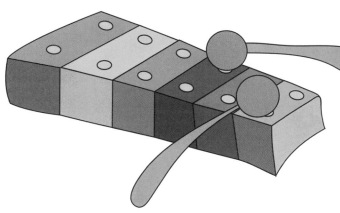

X x

Xylophone begins with the letter X x.

Trace and write the letter X x.

Circle the pictures that begin with the sound of X x.

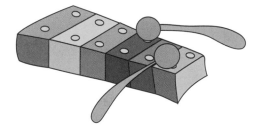

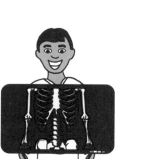

WEEK 8

DAY 1

Aerobic

Go to www.summerfitlearning.com for more Activities!

Exercise for today
Swimming Scissors
Color the star when you complete each level.

☆ **10-30 Seconds**
☆ 31-60 Seconds
☆ **61-90 Seconds**

WEEK 8

 Numbers and Math - Circle the group in each row that has LESS.

Count the cars.

_____

How many cars?

Trace and write the number 16.

16 16 16

DAY 1

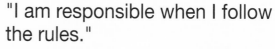

Y y

Yak begins with the letter Y y.

Trace and write the letter Y y.

Circle the pictures that begin with the sound of Y y.

WEEK 8

DAY 2

© Summer Fit   **105**

Exercise for today
Chair Leg-lifts
Color the star when you complete each level.

☆ 1-5 Reps
☆ 6-10 Reps
☆ 10-20 Reps

Be Healthy!
Instead of a sweet, try toast with cream cheese or peanut butter!

Patterns - Look at the patterns below. Circle what comes next.

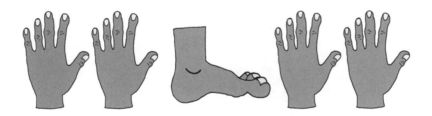
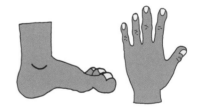

WEEK 8

DAY 2

Responsibility in Action

"I am responsible when I admit I am wrong."

Color the star if you were wrong and admitted it today.

Z z

Zebra begins with the letter Z z.

Trace and write the letter Z z.

Circle the pictures that begin with the sound of Z z.

Exercise for today
Stepping Up
Color the star when you complete each level.

☆ **10-30 Seconds**
☆ **31-60 Seconds**
☆ **61-90 Seconds**

Be Healthy!
Instead of potato chips, try POPCORN!

WEEK 8

DAY 3

Numbers - Trace the number and number words and draw lines to match.

Example:

1   ★★★   two

2   ★★   three

3   ★   one

4   ★★★
            ★★   five

5   ★★
            ★★   four

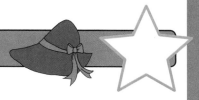
Draw a line to match each set of rhyming words.

Example: Dog
rhymes with Frog

WEEK 8

DAY 4

Exercise for today
Giraffe Walk
Color the star when you complete each level.

☆ 1-5 Reps
☆ 6-10 Reps
☆ 10-20 Reps

Be Healthy!
Take a walk with your parents today.

WEEK 8

DAY 4

Numbers and Math - Add one more.

 +  =

How many?

2
_____

one   plus one   equals two

  =

How many?
_____

 + =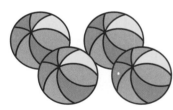

How many?
_____

 =

How many?
_____

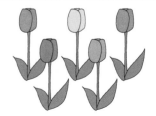 =

How many?
_____

© Photo courtesy of the Terry Fox Foundation

Responsibility is to do the things you know that you should.

Terrance Stanley Fox

Terrance Stanley Fox was a great athlete. Terrance got cancer and lost his leg but didn't let that stop him. He got an artificial leg and learned to run on it. Terry felt it was his responsibility to help others who had cancer too. He started an annual event called "Terry's Run" to earn money for cancer research

www.terryfox.org

Being responsible means I do what I need to do, keep my promises, and admit my mistakes.

Draw a check (✓) under each picture that is showing responsibility and an (✗) under each picture that is not.

_____

_____

_____

"Believe in yourself!"

Choose 1 or more activities to do with your family or friends. Color today's star when you are finished. Good job!

☐ Make a poster showing all the ways you can be responsible for your health and safety....wearing a seatbelt, wearing your helmet, washing your hands, brushing your teeth etc.

☐ Make a chore chart with your parents. Get a sticker each time you are responsible for doing your chores.

☐ Help take care of the earth. Go on a garbage walk with your family to collect trash. Help clean up your neighborhood or park.

Core Value Book List
Read More About Responsibility

The Biggest Bear
By Lynd Ward

Katy and the Big Snow
By Virginia L. Burton

The Empty Pot
By Demi

Reading Extension
Activities at
SummerFitLearning.com

Let's Talk About It

When teaching your child ways to be responsible at home and away show them how to do what is expected. Age-appropriate chores are a great way to teach responsibility. Be consistent with your expectations and praise your child when they complete tasks. Encourage attempts to be responsible and as always set a good example.

Play Time!
Choose a Game or Activity to Play for 60 minutes today!

YOU CHOOSE

Write down which game or activity you played today!

Be Healthy!
Plant a family garden and eat what you grow.

Watch exercise videos at www.summerfitlearning.com

PARENT GUIDE WEEK 9

Skills of the Week

Perseverance

✔ The letter E
✔ The letter A
✔ Sound of sh
✔ Sound of ch
✔ Short I
✔ Letter Uu
✔ Letter Oo
✔ Vowel sounds
✔ Days of the week
✔ Counting coins
✔ Finish the pattern
✔ Missing numbers
✔ Subtraction
✔ Shapes
✔ Draw the time

Bethany Hamilton

Perseverance means not giving up or giving in when things are difficult. It means you try again when you fail.

Sometimes it is easy to forget that a lot of things in life require patience and hard work. Do not give up because it is hard to accomplish a task or to get something that we want. Focus on your goal and keep working hard. It is through this experience that you will accomplish what you want.

Play Every Day!

Weekly Extension Activities at SummerFitLearning.com

Perseverance In Action!

Color the star each day you show perseverance through your own actions.

WEEK 9

Color the ⭐ As You Complete Your Daily Task

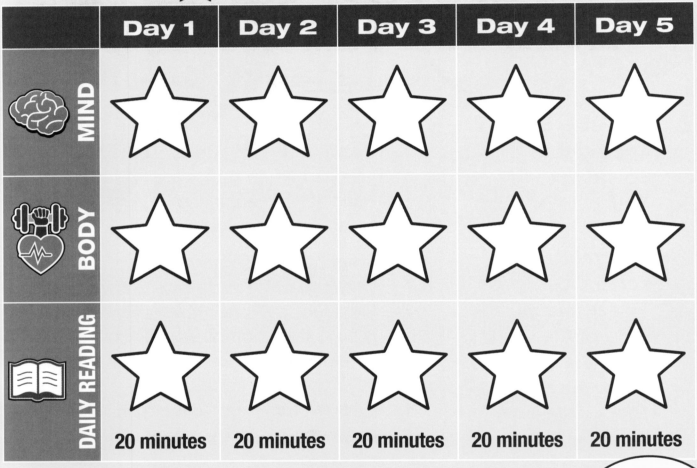

		Day 1	Day 2	Day 3	Day 4	Day 5
🧠	MIND	☆	☆	☆	☆	☆
🏋	BODY	☆	☆	☆	☆	☆
📖	DAILY READING	☆ 20 minutes	☆ 20 minutes	☆ 20 minutes	☆ 20 minutes	☆ 20 minutes

"I have perseverance"

"You Can do It"

_____

Print Name

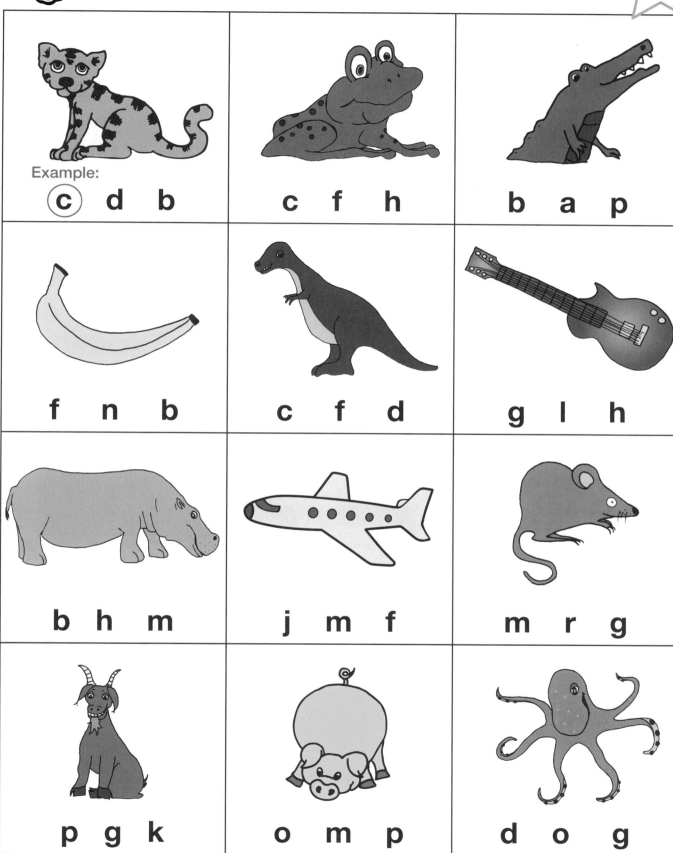

Example:

(c) d b

c f h

b a p

f n b

c f d

g l h

b h m

j m f

m r g

p g k

o m p

d o g

WEEK 9

DAY 1

Exercise for today
Hill Run or Jog
Color the star when you complete each level.

☆ **10-30 Seconds**
☆ **31-60 Seconds**
☆ **61-90 Seconds**

Be Healthy!
Try a new food today.

 Numbers and Math

Write your phone number.

(_____) _____ - _____

Practice dialing your number on the keypad.

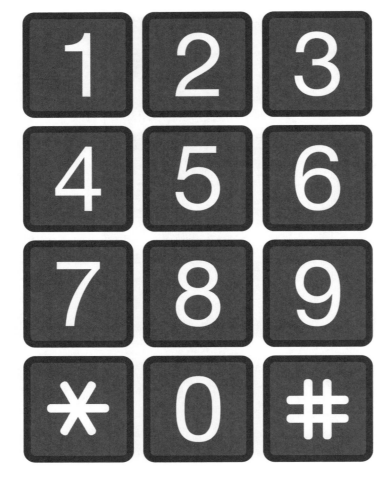

Aa Bb Cc Dd Ee Ff Gg Hh Ii Jj Kk Ll Mm

Nn Oo Pp Qq Rr Ss Tt Uu Vv Ww Xx Yy Zz

Print out the lower case letter for each upper case. Say the sound each letter makes as you write it.

A _____ B _____ C _____ D _____

E _____ F _____ G _____ H _____

I _____ J _____ K _____ L _____

M _____ N _____ O _____ P _____

Q _____ R _____ S _____ T _____

U _____ V _____ W _____ X _____

Y _____ Z _____

WEEK 9

DAY 2

Exercise for today
Bunny Bounce
Color the star when you complete each level.

☆ 1-5 Reps
☆ 6-10 Reps
☆ 10-20 Reps

Be Healthy!
Brush your teeth twice a day.

WEEK 9

DAY 2

1+2=3

Math -

Trace the number word and draw.

 _____

six _____

two _____ _____

  _____

  _____

Example:

WEEK 9

DAY 3

Exercise for today
Hi Yah
Color the star when you complete each level.

☆ **10-30 Seconds**
☆ **31-60 Seconds**
☆ **61-90 Seconds**

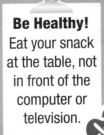

Be Healthy!
Eat your snack at the table, not in front of the computer or television.

WEEK 9

DAY 3

 Full or Empty

Circle "full" or "empty" to describe the pictures and fill in the full and empty text in complete lines.

Example:

full empty

full empty

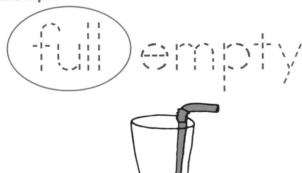

full empty

full empty

full empty

full empty

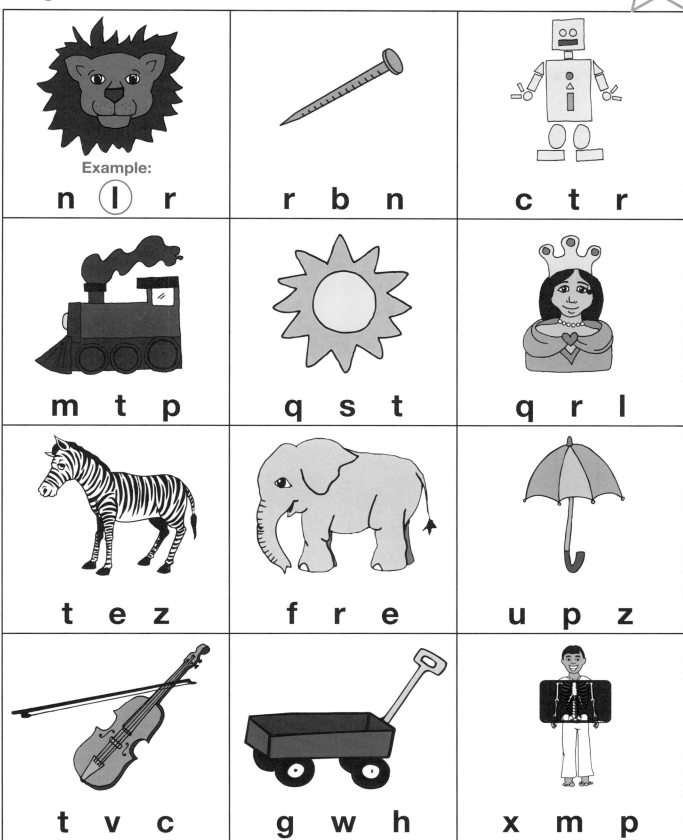

Example:

n (l) r

r b n

c t r

m t p

q s t

q r l

t e z

f r e

u p z

t v c

g w h

x m p

Strength
Go to www.summerfitlearning.com for more Activities!

Exercise for today
Crab Kick

Color the star when you complete each level.

☆ **1-5 Reps**
☆ **6-10 Reps**
☆ **10-20 Reps**

Be Healthy!
Farmer's Market sells local produce.

Shapes - Color and count the shapes.

Triangles = green, Rectangles = blue, Circles = black, Squares = red.

Count how many of each. Write the numbers below.

_____ triangles _____ squares _____ circles _____ rectangles

Circle the hand on the left.   **Underline the foot on the right.**

WEEK 9 **DAY 4**

Spoungeworthy Photo by Phil Stefans

Perseverance is trying again and again and not giving up.

Bethany Hamilton

Bethany Hamilton loved to surf. One day, while sitting on her surfboard, a shark attacked. Bethany lost her arm that day but was determined to surf again. After a long recovery and a lot of practice, Bethany learned to surf with one arm. She is a true example of perseverance and not giving up.

Mark the pictures in the correct order: 1, 2, 3.

Sierra is building a sandcastle. It takes patience and perseverance to build a good sandcastle. Mark the pictures in the correct order.

_____   _____   _____

"Believe in yourself!"

Choose 1 or more activities to do with your family or friends. Color today's star when you are finished. Good job!

- [ ] Read the story of "The Tortoise and the Hare" or "The Little Engine That Could". Make finger puppets and act out the story. Talk about how the characters showed perseverance.

- [ ] Learn how to make paper airplanes. Use trial and error to discover the best design.

- [ ] Cut out a paper star and ask your child to name a goal they have. Write it on the star then talk to them about how they will need to persevere to achieve it.

Core Value Book List
Read More About Perseverance

The Art Lesson
By Tommie dePaola

The Carrot Seed
By Ruth Krauss

The Very Busy Spider
By Eric Carle

Reading Extension
Activities at
SummerFitLearning.com

 Let's Talk About It

To encourage perseverance, expect your child to finish what they start. Resist jumping in every time you see your child struggling. Instead, encourage them to keep trying. If they fail at something help them regroup and try again.

Play Time!
Choose a Game or Activity to Play for 60 minutes today!

YOU CHOOSE

_____

Write down which game or activity you played today!

Be Healthy!
Turn off the TV when you eat.

WEEK 10

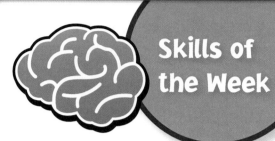

Skills of the Week

- ✔ Long o
- ✔ Long a
- ✔ Long e
- ✔ Rhyming words
- ✔ Long i
- ✔ Long u
- ✔ Missing letters
- ✔ Missing numbers
- ✔ Size comparison
- ✔ Addition and subtraction
- ✔ Counting coins
- ✔ Time
- ✔ Patterns
- ✔ Pairs
- ✔ Count by 5's

Friendship

Lewis and Clark

Friendship is what comes from being friends. It is caring and sharing and being there for each other in good times and bad.

It is fun to have friends that we play with, go to the movies and share our time, but it also is a responsibility. Our friends are people that we trust, protect, respect and stand up for even when it is not easy. We care about our friends and our friends care about us.

Play Every Day!

GET FIT TIME!

Weekly Extension Activities at SummerFitLearning.com

Friendship In Action!

Color the star each day you show friendship through your own actions.

WEEK 1

HEALTHY MIND + HEALTHY BODY

Color the ⭐ As You Complete Your Daily Task

	Day 1	Day 2	Day 3	Day 4	Day 5
MIND	⭐	⭐	⭐	⭐	⭐
BODY	⭐	⭐	⭐	⭐	⭐
DAILY READING	⭐ 20 minutes	⭐ 20 minutes	⭐ 20 minutes	⭐ 20 minutes	⭐ 20 minutes

"You Can do It"

"I am a friend"

_____

Print Name

Rhyme Time - Color the pictures in each row that rhyme.

 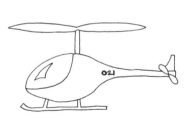  

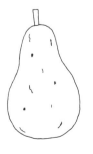   

WEEK 10

DAY 1

Aerobic

Exercise for today
Hula Hooping
Color the star when you complete each level.

☆ **10-30 Seconds**
☆ **31-60 Seconds**
☆ **61-90 Seconds**

Be Healthy!
Tell your family what made you feel happy today.

WEEK 10

DAY 1

🧠 **Compare**

Circle "light" or "heavy".

		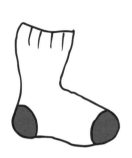	
light heavy	light heavy	light heavy	light heavy

Circle "hot" or "cold".

hot cold	hot cold	hot cold	hot cold

WEEK 10

DAY 2

Strength

Exercise for today
Gorilla Walk

Color the star when you complete each level.

☆ **1-5 Reps**
☆ **6-10 Reps**
☆ **10-20 Reps**

Be Healthy!
Share a joke with a friend.

WEEK 10

DAY 2

Numbers and Math - Count, then trace and write the number.

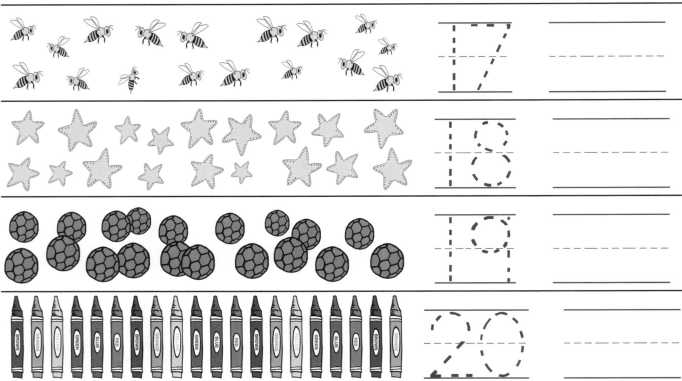

17

18

19

20

Count and write to 20.

1 2 3 4 5 6 7 8 9 10 11

12 13 14 15 16 17 18 19 20

Circle the picture that shows what will happen next.

Exercise for today
Go wild
Color the star when you complete each level.

☆ 10-30 Seconds
☆ 31-60 Seconds
☆ 61-90 Seconds

Art - Draw the missing half and then color the butterfly.

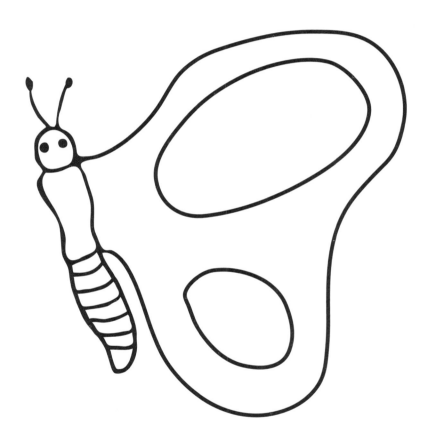

 **Letters and Sounds**

Practice. Write the letter of the beginning sound for each picture.

_____

_____

_____

_____

_____

_____

_____

_____

_____

_____

_____

_____

_____

_____

_____

_____

_____

_____

_____

_____

_____

_____

_____

_____

_____

_____

_____

_____

_____

_____

_____

_____

_____

_____

_____

_____

_____

_____

_____

_____

_____

_____

_____

_____

_____

_____

_____

_____

WEEK 10

DAY 4

© Summer Fit **133**

Exercise for today
Milk Bottle Lifts

Color the star when you complete each level.

☆ 1-5 Reps
☆ 6-10 Reps
☆ 10-20 Reps

Be Healthy!
Smile ☺

WEEK 10

DAY 4

 Numbers and Math - Draw a line to match each set to the correct number.

3

5

10

20

15

8

Friendship is spending time with someone else that you care about.

Lewis and Clark

Lewis and Clark were great explorers and great friends. Together they took a journey across the United States. During their long and dangerous adventure they looked out for one another and stuck by each other even during hard times. They showed us that being a good friend is just as important as having a good friend.

Friends stick together.

Draw a picture of you and a friend. What is something you really like about your friend?

"Believe in yourself!"

Choose 1 or more activities to do with your family or friends. Color today's star when you are finished. Good job!

☐ Make up a puppet show about how good friends act. Also, make a show about what it looks like to not be a good friend.

☐ Make a "Friendship Salad". Gather as many different fruits as you can. With a parent's help, cut up the fruit and mix together to make a delicious salad. Talk about all the different qualities that make up a good friend.

☐ Make a friendship bracelet out of beads and give it to a friend.

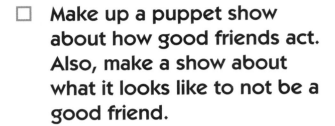

Core Value Book List
Read More About Friendship

Alexander and the Wind up Mouse
By Leo Lionni

Best Friends
By Marcia Leonard

Do You Want to Be My Friend
By Eric Carle

Reading Extension Activities at SummerFitLearning.com

Let's Talk About It

Your child may be nervous about beginning kindergarten, wondering if they will make friends. Talk with your child about his/her strengths and the things that make them a good friend. Role play ways to make friends and what to do when they meet someone new. Talk about how to introduce themselves, how to be a good listener and how to share. Point out that friends can come in all shapes and sizes and to never "judge a book by its cover."

Play Time!
Choose a Game or Activity to Play for 60 minutes today!

YOU CHOOSE

Write down which game or activity you played today!

Be Healthy! Have fruit with breakfast.

Watch exercise videos at www.summerfitlearning.com

EXTRAS
Fitness Index
Family Health and Wellness Tips
Book Report • Flash Cards
Certificate of Completion

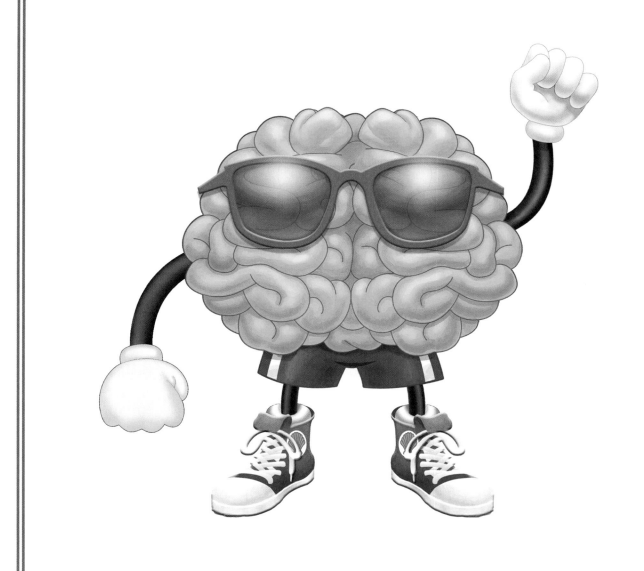

FITNESS 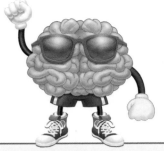 INDEX

A healthy life is an active life. Kids need to be physically active for 60 minutes a day. Use the daily fitness activity to get moving. After 10 weeks of physical activity you have created a new and healthy lifestyle!

AEROBIC

Aerobic Exercise = Oxygen

The word "Aerobic" means "needing or giving oxygen." These *Summer Fit* exercises get the heart pumping and oxygen moving to help burn off sugars and calories!

STRENGTH

Strength Exercise = Muscle

Strength exercises help make muscles stronger. These *Summer Fit* exercises help build strong muscles to support doing fun activities around the house, school and outdoors!

SPORTS

Play Exercise = Sport Activity

Playing a different sport each week is an opportunity to use the *Summer Fit* oxygen and fitness exercises in a variety of ways. There are a lot of sports to choose from and remember that the most important thing about being *Summer Fit* is to have fun and play!

COACH JAME'S CORNER
Hey kids, Have fun moving and getting fit! More training videos at: SummerFitLearning.com

Coach James!
Summer Fit Learning

Warning:

Before starting any new exercise program you should consult your family physician. Even children can have medical conditions and at risk conditions that could limit the amount of physical activity they can do. So check with your doctor and then

Get Fit!

Aerobic Exercise = Oxygen

Aerobic exercises get you moving. When you move your heart pumps faster and more oxygen gets to your lungs. Movement helps burn off sugars and calories and gets you fit!

◆ **Tag:** Decide who is "IT." This person will be the one who chases the others. Everybody will get a turn to be "IT!" Choose the boundaries for the game. If a player crosses the boundaries, he or she is automatically "IT." Players should be given a 5-10 second head start to run. The person who is "IT" should count to that number and then start chasing the others. Every other player's objective is to not get tagged. The player who is "IT" tries to touch another player. Once the player succeeds in doing this, the player who has been tagged is now "IT."

◆ **Foot Bag (need a hacky sack):** Gather players in a circle about four or five feet across. Serve the hacky sack or other foot bag to any player by tossing it gently, about waist high. Keep the foot bag in the air using any part of the body except your arms or hands. Pass the hacky sack back and forth around the circle of players for as long as possible.

◆ **Tree Sprints:** Find two trees that are 10-12 feet apart. Start with your left leg touching the base of the tree. On "go" sprint as fast as you can to the opposite tree, touch the tree trunk, and sprint back to your start position. Continue sprints until you complete your goal or get tired.

◆ **Jumping Jacks:** Start by standing with your back straight and knees flexed. Place your arms at your side. Jump in place, raising your hands above your head and clapping while moving your feet apart. Count 1 rep each time you clap your hands. Continue until you reach your goal or get tired.

◆ **Cross-Country Skier:** Start in a medium crouch position with one leg in front of the other. Lean forward slightly, keep your knees flexed and bounce in place switching your front foot with your rear foot while swinging your arms back and forth with each bounce. Count 1 rep for each time you reach your start position. Continue until you reach your goal or get tired.

◆ **Hide and Seek:** Select an area to play tag. Designate a specific area with clear boundaries. Have everyone gather around a tree or other landmark, which is "home base." The child who is "It" must close their eyes and count to 10. Everybody else hides while "It" is counting. "It" calls out, "Ready or not here I come," "It" looks for the other players but be alert because "It" is searching, while the others are trying to run to home base. "It" tries to find and "tag" the players who are hiding before they get to home base. If they get to home base without being tagged they are "safe." The first player who is tagged will be "It" in the next round. If you all get home safely the same child is "It" again!

◆ **Turtle and Rabbit:** This is a running exercise that you do by running in place. Start in turtle mode by running 25 steps in place very slowly. Then, be a rabbit and run 25 steps as fast as you can!

Watch exercise training videos at: SummerFitLearning.com

- **Wheel Over:** Lie down on your back. Raise your legs off the ground and pretend you are riding your bike in the air. Try to keep your back flat on the floor or ground.

- **Dancing Shoes:** Put some music on and dance, dance, dance!

- **Run or Jog:** Jog or run in your backyard or neighborhood. Pump your arms, keep your back straight, flex your knees, and stay on your toes. Continue for as long as you can or until you reach your time goal.

- **Ghost Run or Jog:** Jog or run in place. Pump your arms, keep your back straight, flex your knees and stay on your toes. Continue for as long as you can or until you reach your time goal.

- **Ball or Frisbee Toss and Run (need a ball or Frisbee):** Start by finding a start place in your backyard or neighborhood park. Toss a ball or Frisbee in front of you 4-6 feet. Walk to pick it up. Toss again 4-6 feet and run medium pace to pick it up. Toss again 4-6 feet and run as fast as you can to pick it up. Repeat as many times as needed to complete your goal or until you are tired. If space is limited, toss back and forth to the same place.

- **Freeze Tag:** In Freeze Tag, one child is "It," and the rest try to keep from getting tagged. When tagged, a child must "freeze" in his tracks until another child unfreezes him (by tagging him or crawling between his legs). When a child is tagged for the third time, he replaces the original "It."

- **Egg Race (need a spoon and egg):** Mark a starting point and a finish point 10-12 feet in distance. Balance an egg on a spoon and race to the finish line! Be careful, don't drop your egg!

- **Swimming Scissors:** Lie down on your stomach. Raise your legs 6-8 inches up and down like scissors cutting through water. Try not to bend your legs and keep your stomach flat on the ground.

- **Stepping Up:** Climb the stairs in your house or apartment. Go slow but see how many you can do!

- **Hill Run or Jog:** Find a hill at a park or in your neighborhood. Jog or run up the hill. Pump your arms, keep your back straight, flex your knees, and stay on your toes. Continue for as long as you can or until you reach your time goal.

- **Hi Yah:** Stand with both feet on the ground. When you are ready, kick the air with one leg and scream, "Hi-Yah!" Now do the other leg. "Hi-Yah!"

- **Go Wild:** Find an area in your backyard or local park. Run, scream, wave your hands in the air, jump up and down – have fun!

Strength Exercise = Muscle

Strength exercises make muscles stronger. When you build strong muscles you are able to lift more, run faster, and do fun activities around your house, school, and outdoors!

◆ **Leg Scissors:** Lie with your back on the ground. Alternate left to right as you raise your legs 6-8 inches off the ground. Stabilize your body with your arms and raise your chin to your chest. Keep your shoulders off the ground. Repeat with smooth, controlled movements.

◆ **Ankle Touches:** Lie with your back on the ground. Bend your knees up with your feet flat on the ground. Alternate from left to right touching left hand to left heel and right hand to right heel.

◆ **Push-ups:** Lie chest-down with your hands at shoulder level, palms flat on the floor, and your feet together. Let yourself down slowly as far as you can go. Straighten your arms and push your body up off the floor. Try not to bend as you push up. Pause for a moment. Then try another one but not too fast.

◆ **Moon Touches:** Stand with both feet together and back straight. Bend your knees and both of your arms in front of your body. Jump straight up with both feet and reach up as you jump with your left and then your right arm. Repeat with smooth, continuous movement.

◆ **Chop and Squat:** Place a solid chair with four strong legs behind you. Start by standing in front of the chair with your legs shoulder width apart and slightly flexed. Keep your back upright. Start with your arms raised above your head. As you slowly squat down until you lightly touch the chair behind you, swing your arms between your legs and clap. Raise your arms back above your ahead as you stand up.

◆ **Fly in the Ointment:** Start by standing straight with your arms stretched out and opened wide. Keep your back upright and slightly bend your knees. Slowly touch one knee to the floor while touching your hands in front of you. Return to starting position and start over by touching the opposite knee to the floor and touching hands in front of you. Complete with smooth, continuous movement.

◆ **Jumping Jacks:** Stand with your arms at your sides. Be sure your feet are straight and close together. Hold your head straight, but in a comfortable position. Bend your knees and jump up while spreading your arms and legs at the same time. Lift your arms to your ears and open your feet to a little wider than shoulder width. Clap your hands above your head. As you return from jumping up bring your arms back down to your sides and at the same time bring your feet back together.

◆ **Jump Rope (need a jump rope):** Start by holding an end of the rope in each hand. Position the rope behind you on the ground. Raise your arms up and turn the rope over your head bringing it down in front of you. When it reaches the ground, jump over it. Find a good turning pace, not too slow and not too fast; however you are the most comfortable. Jump over the rope each time it comes around. Continue until you reach your goal or until you get tired.

"Get Fit! Have Fun!"

◆ **Bear Crawl:** Get down on your hands and feet. Slowly walk forward stretching your arms out as far as you can in front of you. Stay low on all fours and growl like a bear!

◆ **Hula-Hoop (need a hula-hoop):** Start by taking hold of the hula-hoop. Lower it down to about ankle level. Step into it (with both feet). Bring it up to just below your waist. Hold it with both hands and pull it forward so that it is resting against your back. With both hands, fling the hoop to the left so that its inner edge rolls in a circle around your body. Do this a few times so that you get the feel of it. Leave the hula-hoop on the ground for a few minutes and practice your hip movements. Leave your feet firmly planted about shoulder width apart, move your pelvis left, back, right, forward. Do this a few times till you get the feel of it. As you fling the hoop to the left, bring your hips left to meet the hoop and then rotate them back and to the right and forward so that your hips are following the rotation of the hoop. Keep the hoop going around your hips as long as you can. When it falls to the ground pick it up and try again!

◆ **Crab Crawl:** Sit down on the ground with your arms behind you and your legs in front. Move your legs forward followed by your arms. Watch out for any sand traps!

◆ **Rowboat:** This exercise needs a partner! Sit down across from each other with legs spread and feet touching. Lean forward and clasp hands. One pulls forward while the other pushes. Try singing "Row, row, row your boat" while you are exercising!

◆ **Freeze Dance:** Play this with your friends! Put on your favorite music. Everybody dances as hard as they can. One person is in charge of turning the music off – when they do, everybody freezes!

◆ **Snake Curl:** Lie down on your back. Knees bent, feet flat on the ground, and a bean bag between your knees to keep them together. Lay your hands on your side. Curl up and lay back in your starting position. Repeat!

◆ **Chair Leg-lifts:** Place a child-size chair next to you. Standing next to the chair, rest one hand lightly on the back (the back of the chair is facing you). Slowly lift one leg with your knee bent. Now, slowly lower your leg until your foot almost touches the ground. Repeat!

◆ **Giraffe Walk:** Stand up tall with your feet firmly planted on the floor. Keep your back straight and upright. Reach your arms over your head and skip forward twice. Then, slowly walk forward twice again and do another skip.

◆ **Bunny Bounce:** Stand with feet together, knees slightly bent and hands touching your ears. Hop first on your right foot and then on your left. Now, jump with both feet spread apart and then continue hopping, first on the right, then on the left foot!

◆ **Crab Kick:** Get down in a crab position with your body supported with your hands and feet, and your back towards the ground. Keep your seat up and let your body sag. Kick your right leg in the air. After you have done this 5-10 times switch to your left and repeat.

◆ **Gorilla Walk:** Spread your feet apart as wide as your shoulders. Bend at your waist and grab your ankles. Hold your ankles and walk stiff legged.

◆ **Milk Bottle Lifts:** Clean and rinse out 21 quart plastic milk bottles. Fill them with water and screw the caps on tight. Lift them up over your head one in each hand. How many can you do!?

Exercise Activities for Kids

Find What You Like

Everybody has different abilities and interests, so take the time to figure out what activities and exercises you like. Try them all: soccer, dance, karate, basketball, and skating are only a few. After you have played a lot of different ones, go back and focus on the ones you like! Create your own ways to be active and combine different activities and sports to put your own twist on things. Talk with your parents or caregiver for ideas and have them help you find and do the activities that you like to do. Playing and exercising is a great way to help you become fit, but remember that the most important thing about playing is that you are having fun!

List of Exercise Activities

Home–Outdoor:

Walking
Ride Bicycle
Swimming
Walk Dog
Golf with whiffle balls outside
Neighborhood walks/Exploring (in a safe area)
Hula Hooping
Rollerskating/Rollerblading
Skateboarding
Jump rope
Climbing trees
Play in the back yard
Hopscotch
Stretching
Basketball
Yard work
Housecleaning

Home – Indoor:

Dancing
Exercise DVD
Yoga DVD
Home gym equipment
Stretch bands
Free weights
Stretching

With friends or family:

Red Rover
Chinese jump rope
Regular jump rope
Ring around the rosie
Tag/Freeze
Four score
Capture the flag
Dodgeball
Slip n Slide
Wallball
Tug of War
Stretching
Run through a sprinkler
Skipping
Family swim time
Bowling
Basketball
Hiking
Red light, Green light
Kick ball
Four Square
Tennis
Frisbee
Soccer
Jump Rope
Baseball

Turn off TV Go Outside - PLAY!
Public Service Announcement
Brought to you by Summer Fit

Chill out on Screen Time

Screen time is the amount of time spent watching TV, DVDs or going to the movies, playing video games, texting on the phone and using the computer. The more time you spend looking at a screen the less time you are outside riding your bike, walking, swimming or playing soccer with your friends. Try to spend no more than a couple hours a day in front of a screen for activities other than homework and get outside and play!

Health and Wellness Index

Healthy Family Recipes and Snacks

YOGURT PARFAITS: 01

Prep time: 15 minutes
Cook time: 0
Yield: 4 servings
Good for: all ages, limited kitchen, cooking with kids

Ingredients:
2 cups fresh fruit, at least 2 different kinds (can also be thawed fresh fruit)
1 cup low-fat plain or soy yogurt
4 TBSP 100% fruit spread
1 cup granola or dry cereal

Jen Jacobs
Former Contestant of NBC's
The Biggest Loser

It is important to teach children at a young age about the difference between a snack that is good for you versus a snack that is bad for you. It is equally important to teach your kids about moderation and how to eat until they are full, but not to overeat!

YOGURT PARFAITS: 02

Directions:
Wash and cut fruit into small pieces
In a bowl, mix the yogurt and fruit spread together
Layer each of the four parfaits as follows:
Fruit
Yogurt
Granola (repeat)
Enjoy!
Kids can use a plastic knife to cut soft fruit
Kids can combine and layer ingredients

Tips:
A healthier dessert than ice cream
A healthy part of a quick breakfast

SMOOTHIES: 01

Prep time: 5 minutes
Cook time: 0
Yield: 2 servings
Good for: all ages,
limited kitchen, cooking with kids

Ingredients:
1 cup berries, fresh or frozen
4 ounces vanilla low fat yogurt
½ cup 100% apple juice
1 banana, cut into chunks
4 ice cubes

SMOOTHIES: 02

Directions:
Place apple juice, yogurt, berries, and banana in a blender. Cover and process until smooth

While the blender is running, drop ice cubes into the blender one at a time. Process until smooth

Pour and enjoy!
Kids can cut soft fruit and measure ingredients. They can also choose which foods to include.

Variation:
Add ½ cup of silken tofu or ½ cup of peanut butter for extra protein.

PITA PIZZAS: 01

Prep time: 10 min
Cook time: 5-8 minutes
Yield: 2 servings
Good for: all ages, limited kitchen, cooking with kids

Ingredients:
Whole wheat pita bread or whole wheat round bread
Low-fat (part-skim) mozzarella cheese
Tomato or pizza sauce
A variety of toppings: peppers (green, red, yellow or orange), broccoli, mushrooms, olives, apple, pear, pineapple, onions, tomatoes, etc.

PITA PIZZAS: 02

Directions:
Preheat oven or toaster oven to 425°F
Heat pita bread in warm oven for 1-2 minutes
Assemble the pizzas on a cookie sheet:
Spread the tomato sauce on the pita with room for crust
Sprinkle with cheese
Add toppings
Cook pizzas in the oven for 5-8 minutes, or until cheese is melted
Serve immediately with a simple green salad

Kids in the Kitchen:
Kids can choose their toppings
Little kids can cut soft toppings with a plastic fork

Health and Wellness Vocabulary

In order to teach your children the difference between healthy habits and unhealthy habits it is important to know and understand some of the basic terminology that you may hear in the media and from health experts.

Jay Jacobs
Former Contestant of NBC's *The Biggest Loser*

Healthy Websites

www.myplate.gov

www.readyseteat.com

www.nourishinteractive.com

www.cdph.ca.gov/programs/wicworks

www.cdc.gov
(food safety practices, childhood diabetes and obesity)

www.who.int

www.championsforchange.net

www.nlm.nih.gov/medlineplus

VOCABULARY

Calorie: A unit of measure of the amount of energy supplied by food.

Fat: It is one of the 3 nutrients (protein and carbohydrates are the other 2) that supplies calories to the body.

Protein: Is one of the building blocks of life. The body needs protein to repair and maintain itself. Every cell in the human body contains protein.

Carbohydrates: The main function is to provide energy for the body, especially the brain and nervous system.

Type 1 Diabetes: A disease characterized by high blood glucose (sugar) levels resulting in the destruction of the insulin-producing cells of the pancreas. This type of diabetes was previously called juvenile onset diabetes and insulin-dependent diabetes.

Type 2 Diabetes: A disease characterized by high blood glucose (sugar) levels due to the body's inability to use insulin normally, or to produce insulin. In the past this type of diabetes was called adult-onset diabetes and non-insulin dependent diabetes.

Sedentary lifestyle: A type of lifestyle with no or irregular physical activity. It pertains to a condition of inaction.

BMI: An index that correlates with total body fat content, and is an acceptable measure of body fatness in children and adults. It is calculated by dividing weight in kilograms by the square of height in meters. BMI is one of the leading indicators in determining obesity.

Obesity: Refers to a person's overall body weight and whether it's too high. Overweight is having extra body weight from muscle, bone, fat and/or water. Obesity is having a high amount of extra body fat.

Fiber: This is not an essential nutrient, but it performs several vital functions. A natural laxative, it keeps traffic moving through the intestinal tract and may lower the concentration of cholesterol in the blood.

Nutrient dense foods: Foods that contain relatively high amounts of nutrients compared to their caloric value.

Screen time: The amount of time a person participates in watching or playing something on a screen. The screen could be a television, computer, computer games, and a variety of electronics that interact with people utilizing a screen of various sizes. The American Academy of Pediatrics recommends no screen time before age 2 and no more that 1-2 hours of screen time for children over age 2.

Healthly Lifestyles Start at Home

Staying active and healthy is important because it will have a positive impact on every aspect of your life.

Marci and Courtney Crozier
Former Contestants of NBC's
The Biggest Loser

1 **Lead by example:** Your children will do what they see you do. Eat your fruits and vegetables, go for walks and read a book instead of watching television. Your child will see and naturally engage in these activities themselves.

2 **Limit Screen Time:** The American Academy of Pediatrics recommends no screen time before age 2 and no more that 1-2 hours of screen time for children over age 2. Instead of limiting screen time for just them, try regulating it as a household.

3 **Talk at the Table:** Sitting down with the family for dinner gives everybody an opportunity to reconnect and share experiences with each other. Limit distractions by not taking phone calls during dinner and turning the television off.

4 **Drink More Water (and milk):** Soda and other packaged drinks are expensive and contain a lot of sugar and calories. Set an example by drinking water throughout the day and encourage your children to drink water or milk when they are thirsty. These are natural thirst quenchers that provide the mineral and nutrients young (and old) bodies really need.

5 **Portion Control:** There is nothing wrong with enjoying food, but try to eat less. Use smaller plates so food is not wasted and teach your children to tell the difference between being satisfied and overeating.

Healthy Choice Flashcard Game (Following Pages)

Use the Healthy Choice Flashcard games to reinforce good eating and wellness choices. Have a parent or adult separate the flashcards with scissors. Follow the dotted line. Have fun making healthy choices!

Find the two identical objects as quickly as possible. Lay all of the cards face down (Brain Up). Flip over the cards two at a time and try to find a match. If time runs out the game is over, so hurry up!

Reading Recon Preschool

Title of book: _____

Author: _____

Illustrator: _____

Parents: Read or tell your child a story.

Draw a picture of your favorite part of the story:

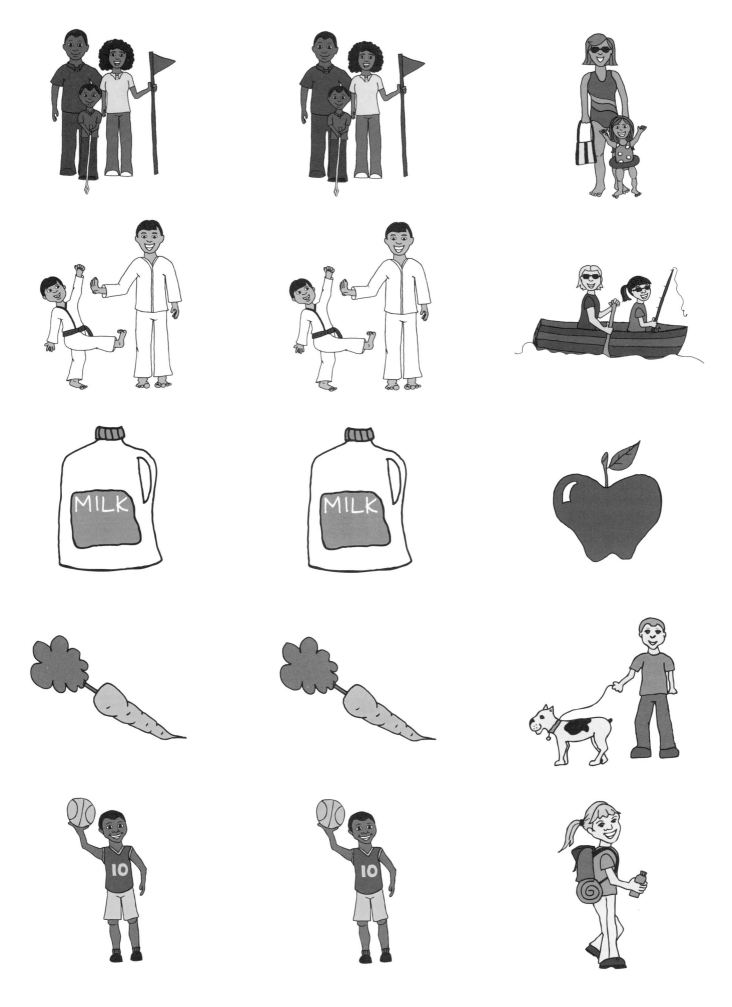

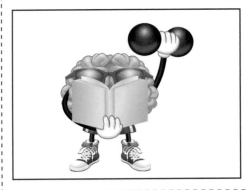

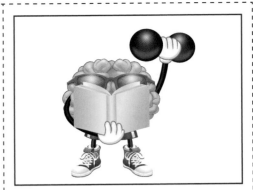

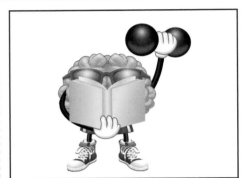

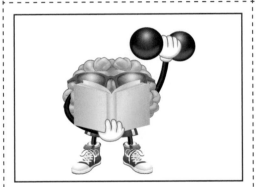

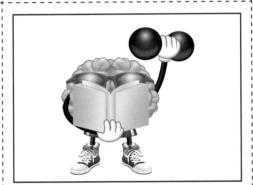

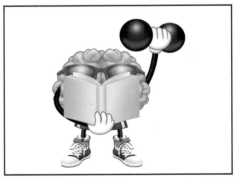

 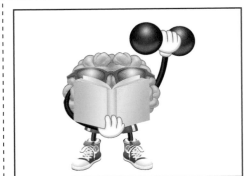 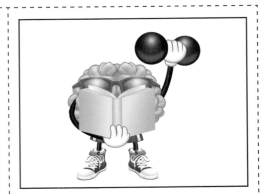

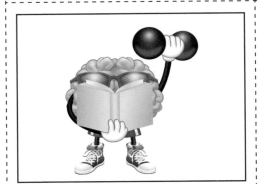  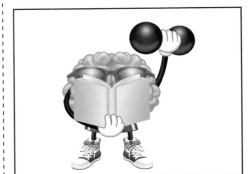

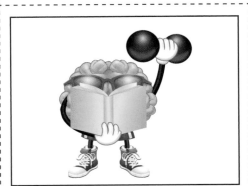 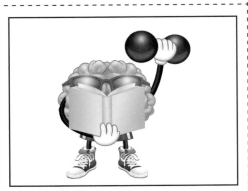 

 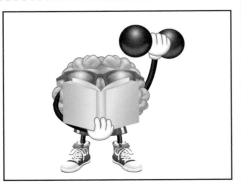 

Aa Bb Cc

Dd Ee Ff

Gg Hh Ii

Jj Kk Ll

Mm Nn Oo

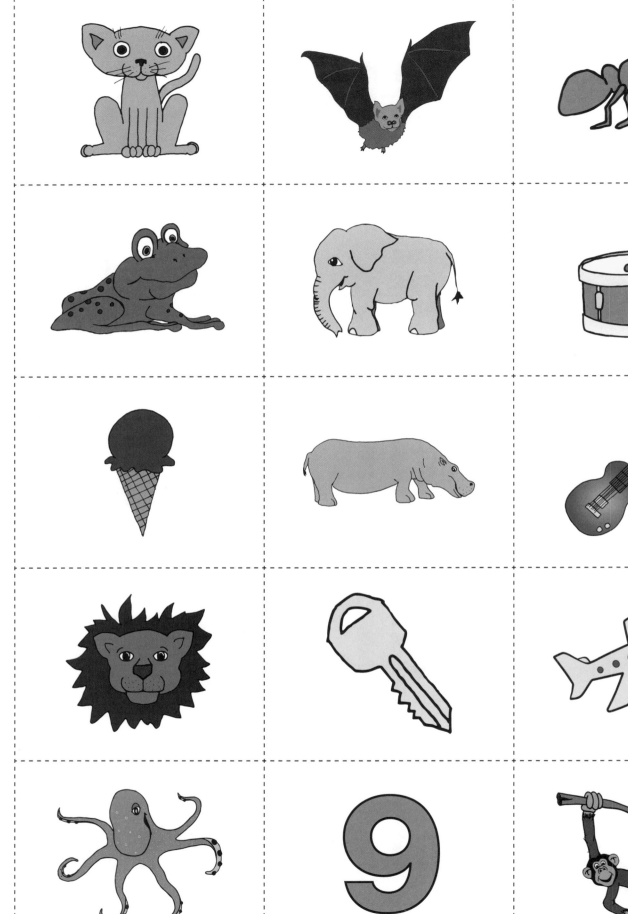

P p Q q R r

S s T t U u

V v W w X x

Y y Z z

1	2	3	4	5
6	7	8	9	10
11	12	13	14	15
16	17	18	19	20
21	22	23	24	25
26	27	28	29	30

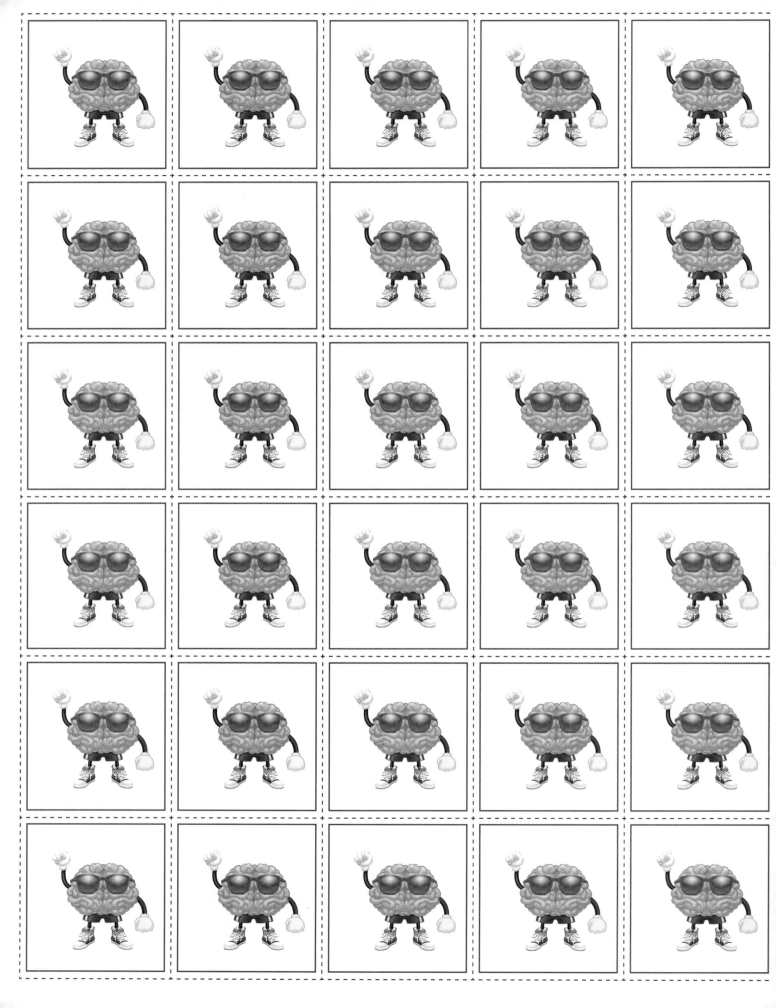

CONGRATULATIONS!

your name

Has completed
Summer Fit!

and is ready for kindergarten!

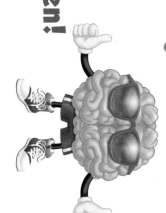

_____
Parent or guardian's signature